MW00355874

My Father & I

By Stephanie Cozzolino

© 2016 Stephanie Cozzolino
All rights reserved.
ISBN: 0692654402
ISBN 13: 9780692654408

TABLE OF CONTENTS

DEDICATION:

To my Heavenly Father who is the best father a girl could ask for. For my Uncle Chaco, thank you for being a key father figure in my life. I will always cherish the memories I have of you and the wisdom you poured into my life. Until we meet again, rest in Heaven.

November 16, 1953 – January 29, 2016

ACKNOWLEDGEMENT:

I would like to acknowledge some key people who have truly been the hands and feet of Christ in the process of writing this book. Without each of you, this book would not be alive today. I would first like to thank my husband, Anthony, and our four beautiful children, Matteo, Bella, Isaiah, and Victoria. Thank you for your patience the days I was frustrated because pieces of my book were scrambled or deleted. Thank you for letting me stay in the bath tub just one more hour as I wrote while the world around me was full of your voices, laughter, screams and requests for more apple juice. Anthony, thank you for always believing in me and being so open and unashamed of my story... our story. Thank you for always loving me unconditionally. To my mother who is the epitome of a Godly woman in so many ways with a heart of gold, thank you for being my villain. Every good book needs one and in my story, the villain has turned out to be my ultimate hero. I thank God for your encouragement and wisdom through this process. You are a diamond in the rough.

Thank you to my editor, Brittany, you are such a gem. Your inbox was full of emails from me constantly with requests and questions and you always embraced them. You truly understand the purpose of this mission. I couldn't have asked for a more patient, and Godly editor. Thank you for being on my soul-winning team! To my graphic designer, Aaron, I told you it would happen one day! Thank you so much for your patience and I thank God for the gift you have to see the visions that God gave me and bring them alive the way you have for my cover and chapter pages. You are truly gifted and talented. I thank you that some people will solely pick up this book because of the beautiful cover. I know you have a lot more where that came from, and we're gonna tap into it!

To my birthing partner, Amber, my sister-in-love, thank you for your constant encouragement, for being so unselfish and always seeing the best in me and always believing in me. Thank you for holding me accountable to the vision that God gave me. Your words helped push this baby out of me. To my family, immediate and extended, I love you all and I pray that you receive the bigger purpose of my story. I thank God that he gave me each of you.

To my readers: Every tear, frustration, anger and trigger was worth reliving in order to reach each of you in one way or another. Thank you for your support. My story is not over, stay tuned

FOREWORD

"Love you too!" These three words have so many definitions when it comes to the relationship Stephanie and I have. We can be talking and out of nowhere, she will get this sudden burst of energy (like she's five again), then blurt out, "Love you too!" It's so funny to see, but I adore when she does it. I'm taken back in time to when my little girl's light shined brighter than the stars. We both smile, I reply back with, "I love you too," and we just pick back up where we left off.

I share this because it testifies to the true power of love and forgiveness. In *My Father and I*, you will read that I am the villain in my daughter's life. As much as I cringe thinking about the world knowing our personal business, I'm constantly reminded by our Lord that somewhere out there in this vast universe we live in, there is a child, mom, or abuser who needs to read what Stephanie has to say. If it helps a child to speak up, a mom to get the strength to do the right thing, or abusers take long, hard looks at themselves and want to change, then who am I to stand in the way of God's ultimate plan?

I have heard over the years that "God takes our test and makes it a testimony, our mess and makes a message out of it, and turns our trials into triumphs." When you read *My Father and I*, you are going to see these three truths play out. Praise be to God that Stephanie has triumphed! At times, you will want to put the book down because it can make you quite angry, but I implore you to keep reading. The good parts are coming, and you will get to read the victory Stephanie has received. My prayer for you is that God will minister specifically to you. We each need to experience the unconditional love that our Heavenly Father has for us. I pray that all unforgiveness will become part of your past, and that you will walk in righteousness and restoration. I also pray for peace to come over your spirit when things become overwhelming. You have run long enough. Now is your appointed time to get your life back, in Jesus' mighty name, Amen!

I want to leave you with 1 Peter 4:8, which says, "Most important of all, continue to show deep love for each other, for love covers a multitude of sins." There is no sin that you have committed that God cannot forgive you for. I'm His living proof. Stephanie, I am so honored to be your mommy. I truly thank you for forgiving me for not protecting you as I should have. You are going to do amazing things for our Lord and leave a legacy worthy of your children to follow. Best wishes and may this book travel all over the world to parts you may never get to go. Love you dearly.

Isaiah 61:1

The Spirit of the Lord God is upon me, because the Lord has anointed

me to bring good news to the poor; he has sent me to bind up the

brokenhearted, to proclaim liberty to the captives, and the opening of

the prison to those who are bound;

One of the most influential relationships that you can have is with your father. It will mold you and have an impact on the person you become while setting the temperature of all other relationships that follow. If your experience with your earthly father is full of pain, rejection and disappointment, then until you receive a revelation of God's heart and unconditional love for you, it will have a negative impact on how you view your Heavenly Father. He is not like anything negative of this world that we may have experienced.

God is a gracious and faithful father that desires a real relationship with His children – a relationship where time is spent in His presence, a mutual love and friendship. He wants to walk beside you, leading you into every great thing that He has for your life. You are full of purpose, destiny and greatness! *My Father & I* is a few chapters out of the book called my life. You will find stories of peace, storms, joy, heartache, revelation, tests, testimonies, forgiveness, and greatest of all, the love and redemption that I received from my Savior, Jesus Christ. The testimony of what God pulled me out of doesn't define who I am, but serves as a testament to God's grace and mercy that immersed itself in and around my life. Our relationship with God has nothing to do with how great we are or aren't, but has everything to do with who He is and how He loves us. God's Grace continuously washes away my impurities while healing my wounds. I invite you to go on this journey with me; a journey that will, at times, be painful yet so freeing. As you read this book, you may cringe, but I pray that you might also know by the end that there is victory because God said, IT-IS-FINISHED. My desire for sharing my story with you is to give YOU the comfort of knowing that you are not alone and you too can come out of any circumstance that was meant to take you out. But that is just the beginning. Knowing that you're not alone is great, but simply not enough. In order to fully overcome, you have to come face-to-face with the things that may have hurt you or stunted you in some way. Many times we also have to deal with the pain we have caused others. Either way, you must bring all of your baggage and burdens to the foot of the cross by surrendering them to God. You don't have to carry the weight any longer. Matthew 11:30 says, "For my yoke is easy and my burden is light."

This process takes time but as you go through it, hold onto God's unchanging hand. Allow God to shine light on all of the hidden and hurt places in your heart. You may even find some that you were not yet aware of. The only thing in this world that can truly make us whole is our father in Heaven. We were made to worship and fellowship with Him. This world is far from perfect and that imperfection, combined with people having free will, allows negative effects to happen that God does not desire for us. Just like God can use someone to bless you, the enemy can use others to TRY to cripple you. I have great news, though! God is love and grace and redemption and freedom. He picked me up off of the ground and out of a pit when I was at a place where I could no longer function anymore on my own with my own knowledge. This was a place where I cried out to Him to rescue me because I was just too weak and hurt to help myself.

Please know and understand that God is not mad at you; He loves you and wants to wipe away every tear and heal every wound. Allow Him to come into your situation, wherever you are or aren't in your life, and He will usher in His marvelous presence. There is power and healing in Him. The same power that spoke this world into existence is the same power that can speak life into anything - and I do mean anything - that you have experienced. God is not surprised, and He is not unaware. He sees all and knows all, so relax in that knowledge by letting Him into even the uncomfortable places - the ones that we don't want anybody to see. It's time to get real with God, He cannot be shocked by you!

Through my surrendering and true repentance, God gave me a new passion for life and a new sense of purpose. I know who I am because I know who my father is. He healed me of my past and gave me hope for a brighter future more than I could have ever imagined; exceedingly and abundantly more than I could ask or think! He can and wants to do the same in your life. My story is much bigger than my past and the struggles I had to endure, but most importantly, it's about being the daughter of The Most High King, who is the best father a girl could ever ask for. Enjoy!

Chapter

1

Surprise

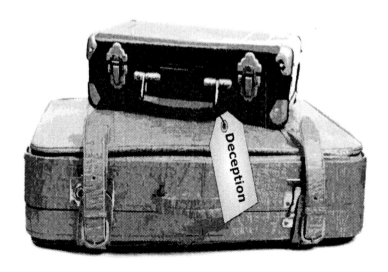

Jeremiah 29:11
For I know the thoughts that I think toward you, says the Lord,
thoughts of peace and not of evil, to give you a future and a hope.

My story begins with my earthly father. He was an innocent child, born into a blended family that would go through trials and tribulations that no one was prepared for. Let me explain: He, along with his identical twin brother, would grow up to become two completely different products of their environment. One characteristic my father had that was both obvious to the naked eye, and masked behind a dimpled smile, was his catchy way of speaking and a presence that could draw anybody in and make them want to be around him, even speak like him. When I think about it, it's actually a gift to have that type of influential demeanor. It began with my paternal grandmother who also had a pretty eventful childhood - to say the least. After giving birth to her first child early in her teens, and refusing to go to school, she ended up living in a girl's home in Detroit until she was 18 years old. Before being released, she was able to go home on the weekends, and during this time, she met my grandfather. The only problem was that she had another relationship with a man of a different race while she was living in the home.

The issue of race became a problem because my grandmother was Mexican and the man she was with was African American. She wasn't allowed to carry on a relationship with him, so as a result, she broke it off shortly before she was released from the home. However, the relationship with my grandfather continued and she soon found out she was pregnant, with twin boys! They were married soon after. My father's name was already picked out; he would be named after his father. A pleasant surprise, until the day him and his twin brother were born. To everyone's shock they came out a different race than that of my Mexican grandmother and grandfather. It was very obvious that the man who fathered these twin boys was the one my grandmother met while living at the girl's home.

Nobody knows the real story, except for a snapshot from my grandmother to my mother because one drunken night, my grandmother spilled the beans. She began to tell my mother the story about being in a home and the birth of the twins and went on further to say that Andre never knew. My mother attempted to seize the moment and asked, "Andre? What's his last name?" My grandmother then snapped out of her drunken spell to accuse my mother of trying to trick her and that she would never tell her that information. That was the end of the conversation, and the end of any clues as to the true identity of my grandfather. "Andre" doesn't even know that he has a whole other family that exists. He has twin sons, seven grandchildren, and eight great-grandchildren. I've always wanted to know who he is. When I was younger, I did my own detective work by calling the juvenile court systems, detention homes, and talking to family members I thought may be able to help me. I even wrote talk shows like Dr. Phil, Oprah, and Steve Harvey, desperate to know my grandfather, but they were all dead ends. I have always felt like it was the missing piece in the puzzle called my life, even at a young age.

The issue of the identity of my grandfather also became mine. Unfortunately, my grandmother took the information to her grave, never telling my father or uncle who he was. There is only one other person, her sister, who knows his identity. We were told that she would only tell my father if he wanted to know. Problem is…he doesn't. His reasoning is he doesn't want to hurt the only father he knew. I do understand that, and I love my grandfather that raised my dad but would love to have this huge blank filled in. This event alone would affect the path of not only my father's life, but the lives of everyone involved AND future offspring - forever.

After a brief separation, my grandparents got back together and had three more children. Regrettably, my father and uncle suffered the consequences of my grandmother's actions. Even though my grandfather raised them and took care of their needs, they were treated like stepchildren and outcasts by him and his alcoholism. They grew up in a home where their father ruled the house and my grandmother was his servant. She herself was also an alcoholic. My grandmother could only do so much to protect them because she also suffered the same abuse. Growing up, my father was in the military, so we lived in different states. Since my parents were both from Saginaw, we would visit during the holidays. I usually stayed with my mother at my maternal grandmother's house and my father stayed with his family. My mom did not like to be in the environment of their home for too long. My grandmother was very close to my father, you could say without a doubt he was her favorite. She was very jealous and no woman was good enough for her son. It didn't help that my mother was very strong-willed and had no problem voicing her opinion. I believe this was due to years of not having a voice growing up (she was the youngest), and various issues being swept under the rug instead of being resolved.

My grandma was also very opinionated and my mother didn't have a problem putting her in her place. Not a good combination. Many of my mother and father's fights stemmed from my grandmother. She even said once that I wasn't my father's child, but if you look at us together, there is no question that I am his seed. All of this hostility did not set me up for a successful relationship with my grandmother. She would say I acted like my mother and she treated me unfavorably compared to my cousin, who was a little bit older than me. I believe this is why my mother didn't let me spend much time around my father's family; sadly even to this day I don't have a close relationship with that side of my family.

I remember once on one of the few nights I ever spent the night with my father's parents; my cousin, our grandparents, and I were on our way home from a party. We were almost to their house when my grandparents started fighting. My grandfather pulled my grandmother by the hair out of their van (it was pretty high off of the ground), dragged her into the house, and beat her. My cousin, who spent many nights with them, knew the drill. She hurried me into the room we would be sleeping in and shut the door. I was so scared; at that point in my life I don't think I had ever been so scared. I remember the look on my cousin's face: it was blank because she was used to it. Looking back on the situation, it was sad because she loved them, but was so blinded by the reality of what went on in their household. To her, it was okay because eventually it would be over. I, on the other hand, laid in the bed shaking, wondering if we were going to be next. It wasn't like I didn't witness my parents in the ring fighting, but it was the unpredictable nature of the situation that made me nervous around my grandfather. It was awful to hear my grandmother's helpless cries, she yelled for him to stop and I remember her specifically reminding him that I was there that night. He was gone though, the alcohol had taken him to the point of no return and she had to suffer through it until it released him. My grandmother never deserved to be treated that way, no woman did. She had her own issues, one of many being low self-esteem. I never understood how someone could live that way, but I have compassion for her knowing that she didn't feel like she deserved any better.

After that experience, I can only imagine what my father grew up with. No child should ever have to witness that kind of abusive environment. When you're a child going through this type of rejection and abuse, on top of witnessing it on a daily basis, it can do damage in so many areas. What my father experienced in the early part of his life with the father he was given is all he ever knew when it came to having an example of what a father was. The results of his experiences would be evident in his life and the way I would be fathered by him.

Chapter

2

Love... Not at First Sight

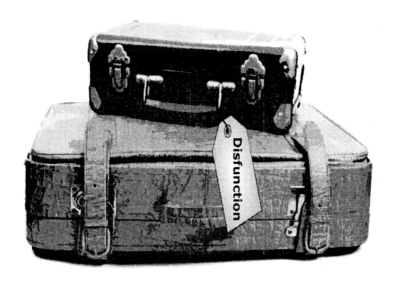

Jeremiah 1:5

"Before I formed you in the womb I knew you, and before you were born I consecrated you; I appointed you a prophet to the nations."

My parents had known each other since elementary age because at one point, they lived on the same street. That's how they met, but it wouldn't be until my mother was 15 years old that she would cave in and go against her better judgment by deciding to date my father. The window of opportunity opened when my father's cousin stood up in my mother's Quinceanera. It is a Mexican traditional dance for young ladies at the age of 15. My father's cousin needed a replacement partner, so in-stepped my father. This gave him the opportunity to get close to my mom and resulted in my father getting his wish, and two very hurt people coming together.

My mother's upbringing was rough, but let's just say the abuse she witnessed and suffered from was in slightly better packaging. My mother was the youngest of eight children and her parents had her late in age, so at that point they were not in their prime parenting years, but did the best they could with the strong-willed daughter my mom was. She had older sisters that took care of her because she was the baby. She also had brothers that would tease her and one that would tell her she was adopted from a pack of monkeys. My mother was darker than the rest of her siblings so she was an easy target for these kinds of jokes. Another brother, specifically, was pretty abusive after coming back from Vietnam. He would hit her, and it would be something she had to deal with – not feeling protected from him. Most of her nieces and nephews were her age, so she was in good company. Even though she was pretty much raised by a village, the unconditional love and attention she needed to thrive was not there. My mom never really felt like she belonged or was wanted. It didn't help that most of her siblings made her feel like she was a mistake because of the age of their parents when they had her. She often struggled with feelings of rejection.

She would spend a lot of time with one of her sisters and her family. During one of the times she visited, my mother's innocence would be breached. She became a victim of sexual abuse by her pregnant sister's husband, her own brother-in-law. She told her mother immediately, but her mother didn't want to come to terms with it so it was swept under the rug, and nobody wanted to deal with it. I believe that her mom and sister knew the truth, but the truth leads you to make decisions, ones that make people uncomfortable. They didn't want to, nor could they handle, dealing with the issue. Abuse is never convenient for anyone - especially the victim. It was a secret, one of the many, which would stay locked up for a time, never coming to the forefront.

On top of everything else, my mother had a strained relationship with her father. He wasn't around much because his main concern was providing for his family, so he worked many hours. He was a very hard worker and great provider, but not very good at relationships, not even with his own children. He too had been hurt as a child; his father was his uncle as a result of his mother being in a relationship with her sister's husband. His mother also died when he was young so her children were left to be raised by other family members. He didn't have much growing up so he didn't want his family to suffer in the same way.

If that wasn't enough, my mother was constantly having to defend herself from words or attitudes that came against her and never quite felt like she had anyone in her corner. Whoever came up with 'sticks and stones may break my bones but words will never hurt me' was not thinking clearly or was much stronger than most. Words are not something that you can take back, and they hold weight. The Bible says in Proverbs 18:31 that, "Death and life are in the power of the tongue: and they that love it shall eat the fruit thereof." My mother would become the black sheep of the family not by choice, but because she felt backed into a corner of rejection and shame. All of the variables of her upbringing created this person that would later rebel and do whatever she wanted to – not always thinking about the consequences. She would make a dangerous pact with herself that nobody would ever take advantage of or mistreat her again. She would become her own boss.

The only problem was my parent's both had the same idea that they were the boss, so they had a shaky relationship from the beginning. Although they had different experiences, the underlying hurt they felt caused the similar pain resulting in rejection and feeling as though they had no control. As a result, they felt the need to control as much as they could. It didn't help that both of their parents had their own issues about why they didn't want their child with the other and vice versa, but that didn't stop them from being together. For my maternal grandparents, it was the undeniable fact that my father was a different race. For my paternal grandmother, it was simply because she just did not like my mother. They didn't let that stop them because it was something that they could control.   In the meantime, my father made it up in his mind to excel at everything he did. You could call him a type of perfectionist. He joined the military to find a way out of the craziness of life, and to have a career. He would always be successful because of his motivation, demeanor, good looks, and charm. His twin brother, however, was quite the opposite. He got into a lot of trouble and, although he could also light up a room, his ambition and determination were lacking. He would try to make some headway, but would continue to relapse.   My parents were not bad people, but they were hurt people and as a result they continued to hurt each other and others. They had good intentions and I believe that they wanted to do better than their parents did. The only problem is when you lack something like a father's love, acceptance, touch and blessing, you are stunted in that area of your life until you get a revelation of the Heavenly Father's love, acceptance, touch, and blessings. You cannot give someone something that you don't have. If you live on a tropical island, you can't make snow balls!

My mother had become rebellious and looked for a way out of her current situation. She ran away to California to be with my dad. My parents decided to finally take the plunge, and they got married on July 6, 1984. It almost didn't happen because my mother tried to leave before the ceremony began, but a friend of hers talked her out of it. Thank God she did, because she would soon find out that she was already pregnant with me. He would soon be deployed after they got married so she made the decision to go back to Michigan to get her diploma and give birth - close to her family. Her father didn't know that she was pregnant until he saw her getting off of the plane at the airport with her pregnant belly, but what could he do? She was already married to my father.

My father missed my birth, arriving shortly after and only able to stay for a week before he headed back on deployment again. It would be six months before I saw him again. My mom said that when he came back at that time, I didn't want anything to do with him because I didn't know him. I believe that this period in time is especially critical for a father to bond with his child because the mother has carried this precious gift as the father has watched on, but this is when he has the opportunity to embrace and plant his very first seeds of love into his child's life.

After my father left to go overseas, my mother would send him pictures of me, but it's not quite the same as spending time with a child face-to-face. As a result, I would spend a large part of my life searching and yearning for the love and acceptance of my father, not quite feeling wanted or accepted by him. It didn't help that I was also caught in the cross fire of my parents' rocky relationship. With their history of hurt and pain, it wasn't a surprise that their marriage was full of physical and emotional abuse, the generational curse of alcoholism, and my father's constant infidelity. I even remember him taking us to the houses of other women while my mother was at work. I remember them very well; one even bought me a doll once and taught me how to braid hair.

My mother wasn't the only one in a battle zone; my little brother and I grew up in it as well. My little brother was born into our family when I was three years old. He was always a daddy's boy. My dad favored him from the day he was born. That was not the case for me. My father was abusive toward me; I remember one time my father was upset and threw a glass baby bottle right at my forehead. I still have the scar today. I can remember the physical fighting and the verbal abuse that was a constant in our home. I was always scared and on edge. I never knew exactly when a fight would break out. My father had inherited his parents' alcohol addiction and this would be the root of many of our household fights, as well. My father was a violent drunk; his abuse would be amplified as each beer went down.

We lived in a total of three states while my dad was in the military. While living in Virginia, where my brother was born, my mother had gotten to the point where she worried so much because she couldn't trust or depend on my father to care for me while she worked because of his drinking and unfaithfulness. When I was three years old, my mom decided to hire a teenaged neighbor girl that lived down the street from us on the military base. She also had some brothers that she took care of. Even though I was young, I can still remember her molesting me. I didn't have a clue at the time exactly what was happening to me but I would later have flashbacks of moments with her that I wish I never remembered. I don't know how long this abuse went on for exactly, but I do remember the moment when it ended. One day my mom picked me up from her house and I had a hickey on my neck. I don't remember getting the hickey and I didn't even know what that was at the time. I just remember my mom looking at my neck and showing my father and her being very concerned. I vaguely remember looking for what all of the concern was about on my neck area and I saw it, there was a dark mark on my neck when I looked into the mirror. My mom never let her take care of me again, even when she would come by and offer to do so. My mom wanted to say something but because her dad was my dad's boss, he didn't want to ruffle any feathers so it was never brought to light. Thankfully at the commissary, a grocery store on the military base, my mom had a coworker named Dee whose parents took over taking care of me, sometimes even for free. I called them Grandma Sheila and Grandpa Willie. They would take me to church without my mom realizing it at first. They were Heaven sent! I have nothing but great memories and feelings when I think about the time that I spent with them. Once we moved and I was old enough, my mother would continue to find churches for me to attend, and even though she herself didn't go, she would make sure I went and would drop me off. These were peaceful times and even though my home was so divided, God made sure that the necessary seeds were planted inside of me. I hid them deep in my heart; He's showing me that even as I write this book. I thank God for using my mom to get me what I needed at that time in order to persevere.

Once we left Virginia, my father was stationed in Missouri. I remember one evening after church I was expecting my mother to pick me up, but it was my neighbor instead. I asked why my mother didn't come, but he didn't answer me. When we pulled into the apartment complex, I saw police cars and ran up to my apartment immediately. Sure enough, my father was going to jail and not just overnight this time but for a few days. As I looked in, feeling sorry for him, it tore me up inside. Even though I witnessed and even fell victim to his abuse, I still felt bad for him and an overwhelming feeling of guilt tried to consume me. It was way too emotional for any child to try to take in.

We lived in an apartment complex in Missouri and my mother found a neighbor who took care of my brother and me. She was so awesome; she was a lifeline for me. She was a single woman, very quiet with a riot of a sister and brother-in-law. The most important thing was that they loved and accepted me. They called me Connie Chung who was a famous reporter because they said I asked so many questions - as in too many, I suppose. Even when Pam wasn't being paid to take care of me, she would still take me places and give me M&M's, she loved them and bought them by the bags; the huge bags!

Nothing good ever lasted too long, darkness always had to peak its ugly head out. One night, when my neighbor was watching me, my parents came back home and my father was being abusive towards my mother. My neighbor pulled a knife out on my dad and I remember screaming for her not to kill him. I was horrified and looking back on the situation now; I think I know how she felt. She was tired of the stories, the bruises, and what we had to go through as kids. I really believed that night that she would have killed my father if my mother hadn't stopped her. I think he knew that too. He steered clear of her after that. After years of abuse and dysfunction, my parents were inevitably divorced when I was the age of seven. It was not my father's choice by any means. He had a really hard time dealing with the divorce, and the fact that my mom had given up any hope of restoring what little love they ever had. It was the definition of when a woman's fed up. Neither of them were perfect by any means of the word. My dad became angry which was soon magnified by the discovery of my mom's new relationship. To say the least, my relationship with my father would continue to be a shaky one.

Chapter

3

The Fill in Father

John 16:33

" These things I have spoken to you, that in Me you may have peace. In the
world you will have tribulation; but be of good cheer,
I have overcome the world."

Both of my parents were later remarried to other people. The kicker was that I was not at either of my parents' weddings, and as I reflect on that, I see how that made the younger me feel even less a part of my family and more rejected. I just couldn't catch a break! Neither of my parents felt it necessary for me to be a part of what's supposed to be one of the happiest times in life shared with the people you love the most, at least that's how I would feel on my wedding day.

When I first met my soon-to-be stepfather, I really liked him. I remember the first time I saw him; my mother brought him with her to pick us up from daycare. I was not expecting it and was really unsure of how to act, but it didn't take long to warm up to him. He took us fun places and bought us cool toys, even when my mother was at work. I can remember him taking us to a nearby lake to feed the catfish. I had never done that before! We didn't do anything extravagant, but it was special to me and I really understood even at such a young age it really is the small things that count to a child. We would also go to a place downtown that had pasta called, The Spaghetti Factory, and anyone who knows me knows that pasta is my favorite food group. I believe that my taste for it sparked from that place. It was delicious! They always brought you out a little cup of spumoni ice cream to finish off your meal. Those were happy memories even if it was only about food.

My life was beginning to change for the better. It was a breath of fresh air because I wasn't used to that type of warm embrace from a father figure. I chalked it up to finally knowing what it was like to have a father that was present and involved. He was giving me the attention that my father had not. My mother really seemed happy as well. I really began to trust him and accept him not only as part of our family, but more importantly, as the father figure I had always dreamed of.

After my parents' divorce, my newly pregnant mother and our new little family moved back to Michigan in December of 1993. It was very cold, and initially we weren't told we were moving back to my parents' home state. We were told, instead, we were going to visit Kentucky; that's where my uncle lived, so we were all for it. That all changed when I saw the Michigan "welcome" sign and quickly blurted out, "Mom did you see what that said?" She was sticking to her story and quickly corrected me by saying I didn't see what I knew I actually had. The cat was out of the bag when we pulled up at my grandparents' house, but at that point I didn't care. I loved my grandparents and missed them so much. Every time we went back to Michigan, I never wanted to leave. I was so close to my maternal grandma. I used to call her from our phone from the speed dial button at a young age just to talk to her. Her home was peaceful and love was there. I felt secure and accepted by my mom's family. After we got settled in, the truth came out...partially. We were told that we had to come back because my father was stalking my mother and due to his abusive past, she was afraid of what he would do. I'm pretty sure my mother's new boyfriend had a lot to do with my father's apparent rage, which was a good enough reason for me. The other part of the truth was that the new fatherly addition to our family would only be staying for a few weeks and then would be moving back to his hometown in California. It didn't make sense because we were just beginning to enjoy having him around, but the fact that he never left would explain all of that. I wasn't too concerned about the deception at the time because it was just great to be back in Michigan. I spent time with aunts, uncles and cousins, and that was something I didn't have the luxury of because we lived out of state. I spent most of the time with my aunt and my uncle that I eventually lived near. They were like my second home. They were a safe haven for me to get away from the chaos of my life and I think it helped my mom, too, because there were four kids in our house. My aunt and uncle loved me unconditionally and poured so many great times into my life. I'll forever be grateful for the refuge I found in their love and acceptance.

Quite a bit of time would go by before I would see my father again, but it was okay, because everything was going great for the time being. When my brother was born, and I was very young, we lived in Virginia, and I didn't quite understand what it meant to have a sibling. But, when my sister was born in May of 1994, I was nine years old and had never loved a little baby so much. I had always wanted a sister. I remember day-dreaming about me driving us around in my car, shopping, and being best friends. She was finally here and she was beautiful, it was better than any doll I could own. All I wanted to do was love her, hold her, look at her, and be near her every second of the day. I loved her. However, things soon changed. I wasn't able to embrace her the way I desired to. I started feeling left out and rejected. I didn't know why this was happening, I didn't understand. When I would try to hold her or be near her I constantly heard my stepfather-to-be say "go over there" or "leave her alone." My brother and I were no longer the priority; actually, it was almost like we were booted off of The Island. Things changed, even in my relationship with my mother. I remember feeling like there was a huge wedge between us and wanting so badly to have her back. I felt like I was competing for her love and attention. Reflecting back, I think I knew exactly how both my father and mother felt growing up. Everything that was good was falling apart right before my eyes and it wasn't even the worst. We lived upstairs at my grandparents' house so we had frequent family visitors. My uncles, aunts, and cousins would all come over and we would be told to "go upstairs." I would feel so left out and angry; after all, they were MY family, not his. I don't remember my mother's voice during this time because I don't think she used it. She would later on and it would be the cause of many fights that would make me believe the lie that everything was my fault.

I remember going on a trip to visit my mom's old friends we considered family in Virginia. I was so excited at first, but the trip went all wrong. I don't remember what I did, but whatever it was resulted in me being put into a dark room the first night there as everyone else was in the house talking loudly, catching up, and having a great time. For whatever reason, this particular incident sticks out in my memory. Something happened inside of me that night; I lost a piece of myself.

Time went on, and because of some fighting at school with girls that didn't like that I talked "white," and boys who wouldn't leave me alone, my stepfather put me in a Catholic school that he paid for. I'll never forget when and how much he paid for things because that's how he explained who loved me and "where my bread was buttered." I used to think about that statement, asking myself, "What does that even mean?" However, I wasn't going to question the man in charge. I liked my school for the most part, and I felt mostly accepted. I don't think the kids had met anyone quite like me. I looked different to them because it was a 99 percent Caucasian school. I was very outgoing, loud and over-talkative. I think talking was a nervous habit of mine, kind of like biting your nails, which I also did. Talking was also an escape from my reality; it was a way for me to cover up my wounds by making people laugh.

I remember starting fifth grade and meeting a girl who was quite the opposite of me. I can't believe she wasn't scared to be my friend! Amanda was my desk partner, and she and her family would later be an amazing outlet and demonstration of love for me. I would go over to their house often on the weekends and have the best time. I always felt right at home, but often wondered why or how they could embrace me the way they did. They treated me like part of the family. I guess I didn't feel worthy deep down. Amanda and I would listen to music and I remember listening to Alanis Morrisette's CD over and over again. "Ironic" was my favorite song, isn't that ironic? I remember my friend's mother making dinner like buttered noodles, peas, and baked chicken. One time after coming home from a weekend at my friend's house, I told my mother about the amazing dinner we had, and not to long after she attempted to make the same dinner. It didn't taste the same, but I was happy because I knew she was trying to make me happy. My friend's mother would also make chocolate chip pancakes and muffins when I was there because I loved them. It made me so happy! Amanda's father was so nice, he was very involved in her life and sporting activities, he was also very quiet but at least he was present. He had huge sunflowers planted in the backyard; I'd never seen anything like them. They were taller than us and the faces of them were so big that you could see each and every one of the hundreds of seeds. They were breathtaking, I've loved them ever since. To this day, every time I see any, I always blurt out, "My friend's father had huge ones growing in their backyard!"

Meanwhile on the home front, my stepfather was always angry and would lash out at my brother and me. He even had a long, thick piece of ribbed green rubber and we called it "the green belt." It was painful to get whooped with that thing; for the most part my mother was the one who hit me with it, but he took care of whooping my brother pretty excessively and quite often. It even had our names on it, my brother's on one side and mine on the other. I never knew what happened to that belt, it was accidentally lost for all I know. The little bit of childhood that I did have would soon be gone in an instant.

When I was in the fifth grade, my mom was pregnant with my youngest brother. It's amazing the way the mind can block traumatic things out of one's memory. This event would forever change my life, in the same way that things changed the day my father and his twin were born. I've tried before to think about exactly when it took place. I've tried to think about the weather outside or what sport I was playing, but I always draw a blank. This part of my life is a black hole.

At my grandparents' house, there were three rooms upstairs. The first was mine that I shared with my brother. You had to walk through ours to get to the next one, which was my stepfather's and mother's room. The last room at the end of the hall would eventually become mine, but it was originally a large closet. It was late one evening, and my mother was already sleeping. My brother was also asleep on the other side of the room in his bed. My stepfather came out of his room and sat on my bed. He called me over and sat me on his lap. He asked me if I knew how to kiss. I remember being so confused and almost frozen right there in that moment and completely shocked. I didn't know what to say or how to scream, I just sat there, still. He started to kiss me, and when I didn't kiss him back, he said "That's not how you kiss, you're not doing it right," sticking his tongue into my mouth. He then put his hand up my shirt and started fondling my breast. I was still frozen.

When I used to think about this event, I would be angry with myself and ask *Why did I just sit there? Why didn't I scream, my brother was right there and my mother was right in the next room, my grandparents were downstairs!* All of these people were within feet of me, yet nobody could help or protect me from this monster. That's all I remember, I don't know how things ended. It's so sad that something that happens so quickly can cause such lasting damage.

When I woke up the next morning, I found that this event had claimed more pieces of me: my childhood innocence, my ability to trust, and my self-worth. My stepfather was a barber at the time, so he was gone by the time I got up to get ready for school. My mother sat me on her bed with a look on her face that made me feel ashamed, not because she was angry at me, but because I could see the hurt in her eyes, a reflection of my eyes in hers. She asked me what happened the night before, I remember thinking and asking "How did you know?" She said she was able to tell by the way I was acting. Her response never sat well with me, and to this day I haven't asked her again. I started telling her what happened, and when I finished, she hugged me and cried, apologizing to me. Looking back on how things transpired afterward, I wonder if she was crying because I was hurt, or because she knew she would have to choose between him and me.

I don't remember that day at school, apparently I floated through it, but I don't know how I made it with all of that on my mind and the feeling of my body being violated. I was already good at hiding underneath my smile, but I would soon master those skills in order to cope. After school, my mother was there to pick me up. She told me the story of how she confronted my stepfather. She went to the barber shop and he had all of the blinds closed and no customers because she said he already knew she knew what had happened. When she arrived, he was sitting in his barber chair, waiting. She asked him why he did it and then scratched up his face. She never told me what his response was but said he was going back to California where he was from and wasn't coming back. I was so relieved to hear this, despite the dark cloud of what happened to me. This was great news! She asked me how I felt and I told her I hated him, and I never wanted to see him again. She then told me I had to go upstairs and tell him how I felt as we sat in the car outside of my grandparent's home. I told her I didn't want to see him, I didn't want to talk to him, but she made me do it anyway. The only thing that got me up those two flights of stairs was that once I did this, he would be gone forever. I did a walk of shame and went into their bedroom. He was lying on the bed with a pitiful look on his face, silent. That was pretty unusual for him because all he ever did was talk; I think he would do it just to hear himself. I believe he talked for the same reason I did: to hide behind it. I began to tell him how I hated him for what he did to me and that I never wanted to see him again and wanted him to leave. I think my mother intended to make him leave, so I never understood why she made me go up there and face him because it was so painful. Maybe she thought it would help her follow through with it if he heard it from me. I said it with oomph because I knew that's exactly what was about to happen...UNTIL he never left. He continued to live with us in my grandparent's home until we moved into our own home. He wouldn't leave until I was in high school. Talk about pain, fear, rejection, abandonment, loneliness, distrust, and a lack of protection!

The decision my mother made (or didn't make, however you want to look at it) would haunt me for a long time to come. I was confused, hurt and scared. The one person that I just knew I could trust let me down in the worst way possible. I was lost and lonely and couldn't turn to anybody because it was our secret. When I was in my early 20's, I would be seen by a psychologist and told that I suffered from severe post-traumatic stress disorder (PTSD) as a result of my molestation. I knew my mom was molested also, so that outraged me even more. I would think to myself, *you know how much that hurt, especially when nobody stood up and protected you? How could she do that to me?* I would think to myself, *how could she be with someone who molested her daughter and who knows how far it would have went if she would have not asked me about it the next morning?* The thought of it would make me sick to my stomach. Shortly afterward, my mother was in the hospital because my brother was prematurely trying to make an entrance into the world. I believe it was from all of the stress she was under because of what was happening in our family life. She instructed me to sleep downstairs with my grandma while she was admitted to the hospital. I remember wanting to tell my grandma, but my fear of my mother would override any chance of doing that. I was told not to tell anybody, it would have to remain another family secret - for a while anyway.

Chapter

4

The Residue

Psalm 34:18
The Lord is near to the brokenhearted and saves
the crushed in spirit.

My father would soon win visitation rights when I was in the sixth grade and my brother and I would have to go visit him in Missouri where he still lived for six weeks during the summer. Believe it or not, I was nervous, but at the same time ready to get out of my current situation. My parents would meet halfway when dropping my brother and I off and picking us up. I remember feeling like I wasn't going to make it, or live long enough to make it back home. I was lying in the back seat and remember looking at my brother before falling asleep. I said to myself, "I want his face to be the last thing I see before I fall asleep in case I never wake up." Somehow I thought that would comfort me in case I never woke up. I can see the enemy trying to lie to me, telling me that I would die. I used to say, "I always knew I would die young." It was a lie straight from hell! If you knew my relationship with my brother at the time, we fought like cats and dogs. You would be thoroughly surprised that his face would be the last thing I wanted to see.

Because of my history with my father, I found myself a scared little girl again. I felt as though I was walking on eggshells. No matter how hard I tried, deep inside I felt not good enough. I yearned for his love. I craved it. There was a hole in my heart that I wanted my father to fill. It didn't make it any easier, because of the abuse I suffered from my stepfather, it made it awkward to be alone with my father. I knew he would never hurt me, at least not in that way, but I kept a barrier up. I never wanted to feel that pain again. Since my father had remarried, his wife and her two children also lived with them. She was nice, but spent a lot of time prying for information and bad mouthing my mother. I didn't like that at all. She picked at everything I did from hygiene, to how I did my hair, what kind of clothes I wore, or the fact that I didn't wear nylons under dresses. She was a country girl and I wasn't, so I didn't fit inside the box she wanted me to. She was a great cook though, very crafty and involved with her kids. I did like that but not many things made her happy.

My relationship with my father was slowly on the mend. We were working on building our relationship the best we knew how. Music was a start. I loved listening to music with my dad and singing. That's one of my favorite memories of him: Motown, 80's and 90's R&B, and don't forget the slow jams. To this day, I still love all of those songs. I think music was his escape; it made his reality easier because he could get lost in the songs. When I was a little girl and he had a few beers in his system, he would sit me on his lap and sing to me and play the "air piano" as I would call it. It always embarrassed me, but deep down I liked it. I visited for a few summers and enjoyed it for the most part. I also had my step siblings and their friends to have fun with. I got to hang out at the community center, swim all day, and go roller skating which was another one of my favorites. I loved skating to different music; it was another escape from reality because I could get lost in it.

My dad was very involved in his step kids' lives and he coached their sports. I wish I would have had that. At one point, I even wanted to live with my father but that wasn't going to happen, not over my mother's dead body, to be very honest. I remember many times just wanting to tell my father about what my stepdad did to me, but I never even got close. I wished he would have had that talk with me about good touch and bad touch, but it never happened. This was one of those times that I would later look back and say, "Why the heck didn't I say anything, why was I so afraid?" Well, it's not that easy when you're in the chaos and so young. I felt like it was me against the world; I didn't trust anyone. I didn't trust that if I did tell him, he would be able to protect me.

The sad part is that the shame causes you to feel guilty, even to the point where you feel bad for the abuser. It's actually pretty sick, but I would later find out that there is no shame or guilt in Christ. After a few summers, I no longer had to go see my father anymore, which was fine with me. I was getting older and had my own life. My home situation wasn't great so I tried to keep myself busy; I just hung out with friends, played sports and went to sleepovers. I remember at one of them in particular, a bunch of us girls were talking and something was said that made me confide in them about being molested. I always wanted to have someone to confide in other than my mother. She told me some time after the incident that I could talk to her about it anytime, but she didn't really want to face the questions or the hostility that I had toward her. She gave nothing but excuses, which angered me even more, so I told my friends about it, and unfortunately all they did was look at me. I don't think that they understood exactly what that meant. I told them not to say anything, half of me hoping they did and half of me hoping they didn't. They didn't because I never heard another thing about it or they did but nobody knew how to handle that information.

The abuse didn't completely stop; it just got a little less obvious. One day I had a stomach ache and was lying in bed before school. My mother was still in bed and my stepdad came into my room and started feeling around my stomach, then his hand went down towards my "lower stomach" as he asked me "Right there, does it hurt right there?" He would also try to kiss me goodnight, which I have no clue why that was ever even happening in the first place, and would slip his disgusting tongue into my mouth. I don't think I ever told my mother, after all, would it even matter?

When I was in the ninth grade, everything came to a brief halt when my mother found out he was cheating on her with another woman who was married, a woman that he would later get pregnant twice and eventually marry. I remember my mother picking me up from school looking somber and telling me the news. The next few years were a living hell. It was full of slashed tires and embarrassing public scenes. It was basically like World War III. My mother ended up kicking him out. Apparently for her, THIS was the last straw. Unfortunately, he would continue to come around for quite a while after that for special visits with my mom. One evening in particular was pretty bad; he came over and then started fighting with her. My mother threw a glass figurine at his head and he fell to the ground pretending to shake. When he got up he went after my mom so I did what any person trying to protect her mother from a crazy man would do. I grabbed a Little Tykes golf club and started hitting him with it to get him off of her. The fight ended in the front yard with our audience full of neighbors until the police were called to the scene. This would be a regular occurrence during this period of my life.

Chapter

5

Tainted Love

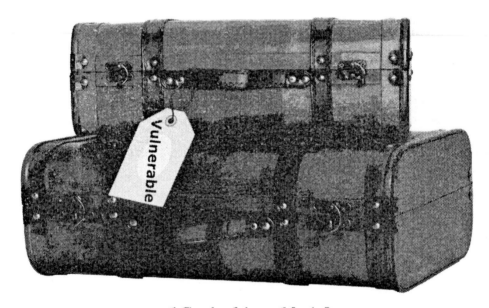

1Corinthians13:4-8
Love is patient, love is kind. It does not envy, it does not boast,
it is not proud. It is not rude, it is not self-seeking, it is not easily
angered, it keeps no record of wrongs. Love does not delight in
evil but rejoices with the truth. It always protects, always trusts,
always hopes, always perseveres.

Surprisingly enough, in the midst of this craziness and drama, I would meet my knight in shining armor. Before Anthony came along, I was boy crazy. I had about four boyfriends in a short period of time. The good news was that my stepfather wasn't at our house full-time anymore, a contributing factor to why I had so many boyfriends. When he was around, I couldn't look at, talk to, or even spell the word "boy." I see it now for what it was: a sick jealousy. He could no longer control me and, as far as I was concerned, I was going to do what I wanted to with who I wanted to.

The day I met Anthony was like any other day. I was 15 years old and a sophomore at a new high school for me. He was 17 and a senior at a different high school. My mother worked, so she couldn't pick me up from school this one particular day, so I had to get a ride from a girl I knew and somewhat got a long with due to past issues. I'm pretty sure she used me as a guy magnet for her benefit. Little did I know, God would use her to bring Anthony and I together. After school one day, we hurried out to her car because we wanted to avoid the other girl she usually gave a ride home to. That failed because she was already waiting for us at my friend's car. On the way to her house, we saw a boy that my friend went to school with before and she stopped at the corner to talk to him. I was ready to go home, but she insisted on us going to his house right around the block after we dropped her other friend off. I wasn't too excited about it but, I also wasn't driving, so I went along with it. We pulled up, got out and talked to him on his porch. All of a sudden we heard, "BOOM, BOOM, BOOM," and in the distance I saw a little black Saturn pulling up with a loud, vibrating stereo system, and out came Anthony! My first thought was, *who is this white boy bumping this rap music?* He definitely caught my attention, but that's about the extent of it. My friend then had the great idea that we all go grab something to eat, even though I was ready to leave when we got there, so we did. I, of course, ended up in the front seat with the boy with crazy loud music. It would be one of many times I would be the passenger in that car. Sometime between eating and getting back to the house, I was asked to go to his homecoming with him that weekend because his date couldn't go anymore. I said what any girl with a boyfriend would say, "Yes!"

A few days before Anthony took me to his dance, the guy I liked came to my house with his friends and they were hanging out in my driveway. Anthony rolled up with his friend and, when they got out of the car, my mother said "What about that one?" She was pointing to Anthony, but I brushed her off. If you ask her now why she said that, it's because she heard it in the Spirit, but at the time she didn't realize it. On the night of his homecoming, we ended up going to dinner at my favorite Italian restaurant before the dance. His friends were really nice and I fit in well with them. When we got to the dance, we didn't see much of each other because I had my own agenda. However, after the dance I found out he did also. He dropped me off and just as I got the last of the bobby pins out of my hair, my pager went off so I called him. His plans for after the dance fell through, so he wanted to know if I wanted to go hang out with him, and I said "No!" I wasn't about to be his backup plan.

The very next weekend was my homecoming and because my friend's date bailed on her, she made me ask Anthony if he would go with her. He was thrilled! I later realized it was because he would once again have the opportunity to be around me. As we sat at dinner and I was with my boyfriend, Anthony was four chairs down from me at the table paging me. I looked down the table when I recognized his funny coded number he paged me in, and he had a huge smile on his face, waving at me. That night was fun and even though my soon-to-be ex-boyfriend was my date, Anthony still tried to steal a dance. At the after party, I was really ready to go home. My friend wanted to stay, so Anthony volunteered to take me home. He was a harmless, goofy guy so I let him take me home. He wasn't like any of the other guys I knew, which was a great thing. I think that my mother appreciated that the most. Anthony would call me later that week to go to a soccer game with him. I thought that was the weirdest request, but I went because my mother encouraged me to go do something different. Come to find out, we went there because he didn't have much money. I think he was a breath of fresh air for her compared to the other guys I had previously dated and I didn't mind being around him.

On Sweetest Day, an old friend, her boyfriend, and I were going to a haunted house and Anthony called as we were getting ready. When we told him our plans, he said he wanted to come along and I said that was fine, why not, right? We met him at his house and all drove together. When he came to the car he had a bouquet of flowers and the biggest teddy bear I had ever received and said, "Happy Sweetest Day!" Up until that moment, I honestly didn't realize that he really liked me or what Sweetest Day even was. He wasn't like the other guys in a lot of ways because he wasn't overwhelmingly forward with his approach. Most guys I knew would ask for my phone number and then my name. Plus, he bought me flowers and a teddy bear. That changed everything and for the rest of the night, I looked at him as a potential boyfriend - not just a random guy that happened to show up at random times. Anthony's family was great and despite our racial differences, they were very accepting. I loved being at his house because it was the opposite of mine. He was the youngest and the only child living at home. He had four older sisters and he was the only boy. Being the oldest of four at my house, along with my mother being a daycare provider, made life pretty hectic. Being at his house was a great way to get away from my house, so we spent a lot of time there. We had a lot of fun together and became inseparable. Anthony was two years older than me, so he graduated in 2001 and enrolled in college. He wanted to be around me every second to the point where he was slacking in college. We would do everything together, and as a result, our lives would soon change.

One of the biggest changes happened a few months after 9/11 while watching playbacks of the event on the news, I had no idea that my mother, brother, and I would be on a plane to New York City to be guests on the Montel Williams show. It was all because of a ladder and some Christmas lights. Let me explain: I never really liked Christmas for a number of reasons. It reminded me of black snow like the snow on the roads that was black and slushy. This year though, I was pumped and we were going to have some holiday cheer. We got some Christmas lights to put up at my mother's house. The ladder we had was pretty old and shaky, so Anthony told me to wait to get on it until he could get over to where I was to spot me. I did the opposite and, as it started to fall, I tried to jump off of it onto a cement landing. Bad choice! I ended up with a huge bruise on my side and a trip to the hospital. I lacerated my spleen and spent a couple of weeks in the hospital and out of school for a month. It was horrible and boring since I wasn't able to do much. I was so bored that one day, as I watched The Montel Williams Show, I saw the title "Are you tired of your parent being lonely on New Year's Eve and you want to hook them up on a date?" Well of course I did, my mother had been through a lot and, after kicking my stepfather out a few years earlier, I wanted her to be happy and I thought a date was just what she needed so I did the most logical thing possible: called the show. I left a message and within a day the producers gave us a call back. I didn't answer the phone when they called, nor did I tell my mother that I had volunteered her to be someone's possible New Year's Eve date. My mother answered and hung up on them thinking it was a joke when they said they were calling from the show. They called right back and before my mother could say anything they pleaded with her not to hang up again and that they really were from The Montel Williams Show. She didn't hang up on them again, but listened. They explained why they were calling and wanted pictures of our family right away. Within an hour, there was a Fed Ex guy at the door. A week later, we were on a plane to the studio in New York City. It was an awesome experience, but since my mother was not ready to date again, nothing came of it other than a free trip to New York, an awesome story to tell, and some really great pizza.

In February, two months later, and a few days before my birthday, my paternal grandmother died, and the hope of me ever finding my real grandfather died with her. She was buried on my birthday and during the funeral I gave a speech, talking about the shakiness of our relationship but that on her death bed we made peace. I knew she understood me before she passed because she squeezed my hand as I talked to her. Not long after that, there was another death and it was Anthony's maternal grandfather. We had some unexpected things come our way. With death there also came life, a very unexpected life.

I would find out at lunch one day during my junior year that I was pregnant. My school didn't allow students to leave during lunchtime, but I found a way out on most days because Anthony had an open campus. I took the pregnancy test at Anthony's house and we were both in shock. We talked about what we would do. Abortion or adoption was never an option for us, so we knew we were going to ride it out together and have this baby. After processing the news, I knew I had to tell my mother, but was afraid of what she would do or say. Things were finally starting to settle down in my life… now this. I was also afraid of how Anthony's parents would react. I didn't really have to declare it to my mother because she guessed it. She came home from shopping one day and I was sitting on the couch with my robe on and a pouty face. She knew me very well and asked what was wrong, thinking that I was upset that she went shopping without me. She then handed me a new bra and said, "Here, I bought you something."

I went up to her and gave her a big hug and cried my eyes out on her shoulder. She didn't even know that I was having sex. She asked what was wrong. I think she thought it had something to do with Anthony, and not just the fact that I was going to have his child and her first grandchild. I said I couldn't tell her, but after a seemingly long pause, she said "You're pregnant?" I said yes, and she asked me what I was going to do and I said I was keeping the baby. I don't remember the rest of what happened, but I know that Anthony had to give her some space for a little bit until she eventually got over it. She was just disappointed and concerned about me finishing school and going to college. I wasn't there when Anthony told his parents, but I'm pretty sure their reaction was similar. The time approached for me to tell my father because after all, he was my father, so he should know. It was awkward telling him since he wasn't too involved in my life, but I did it anyway. He asked me if I was going to have the baby and, of course, I said yes. This growing life would bring new life into our relationship. Our first baby was on the way and we would later learn we were having a boy. Along with the hormones, Anthony and I had a somewhat shaky relationship. We loved each other, but the problem was my definition of love, according to the examples I was given and witnessed while growing up. It was that I didn't really understand what love was or how to have a healthy relationship; I just had a lack of great relationship models in my life. I felt like I had to protect myself. I would always say if anyone is getting abused in this relationship it wasn't going to be me! I grew up watching my mother in abusive relationships and I vowed that would never be my story, so I was willing to fight if I ever found myself in that type of situation. I know that, in turn, I created walls around my heart that were impossible for Anthony to get over. Anthony was no angel and it was hard for me to get over times that he would upset me and I know that had a huge part in keeping things from evolving into a more mature relationship. Two stubborn and selfish people don't make for a successful relationship.

I was not alone when I started my senior year of high school. I had a beautiful baby boy that was growing inside of me and almost ready to make his appearance into the world. I promised my mom that I would finish high school on time and go to college. I assured her that I would work harder to achieve my goals. The day before I was scheduled to have my labor induced (I was a week over my due date), Anthony and I got into an argument down the street from my house that resulted in me making him pull over and letting me out of his car. I walked home that cold November day in 2002 with a big belly waddling down the street. I couldn't tell you what I was upset about, but I can tell you it was probably something really stupid. I couldn't stay mad for too long because the next day I was scheduled into the hospital. After two days of labor with very little dilation I was forced to have an emergency C-section on a Thursday. Although my experience was long and tiring, nothing could take away the fact that it was the most amazing day giving birth to my first child. I cried when I saw him. It was love at first sight. He was worth every piece of muscle that they had to cut through! He was such a big boy and the most precious thing I had ever laid eyes on. That little boy saved me. I always said I was going to be on the show called "The Real World," and I just knew I would be famous but for all of the wrong reasons I'm sure. I don't know what direction my life would have gone if I didn't have him to love and take care of. My father made sure that he was there to visit his first grandchild on the day he was born, which meant a lot to me. As I watched him with my son, I was happy that even though he wasn't there for me the way I hoped, I was glad that he was attempting to be a great Papa.

Anthony and I would have our good times and bad, but it would be like a slow leak of helium out of a balloon. Seven months after I had our son, I graduated on time with the help of a home school teacher that would come once a week and hand in all of my work for me. Without that program my school provided, I wouldn't have graduated on time that year. I was able to do my work in between taking care of our son. I accomplished what my mother had been concerned about and I was proud of myself.

The next fall, I enrolled in college and began taking classes. Anthony and I had always both worked, so when it came to providing for our son, we made it work. In March 2005, I got pregnant again, but on April 1, I had a miscarriage. The emotional pain from the miscarriage was awful. I wasn't far enough along to know the baby's gender, but that was still my baby and I was a wreck. I cried and cried and cried some more. I remember my mom coming to my town house with a new bed spread and moved my room around to try to make me feel better. Even though that pregnancy wasn't planned, deep down I grew a desire to have a baby after being pregnant and miscarrying. I think subconsciously I didn't do everything I needed to in order to prevent another pregnancy and so, a few months later in July, I found out that I was pregnant again. I was so happy but a little nervous about what Anthony's family would say.

In September of 2005, my father came to visit me. I was only a couple of months pregnant at that time with our second child. Ever since I had my son, he was pretty involved and he would visit a few times a year and spend time with him and buy him things he needed. He truly he was a great Papa. Even though my parents were exes, they still had a long history together and at the very least, they had their kids and now grand children in common. It was not abnormal to have my mother and father hang out while my dad was in town visiting from his home in Missouri. My mom had no romantic feelings for my dad and I think my dad would allow beer to take him back to the old days. One night, we were at my house having dinner and I remember specifically that I made lasagna. We were sitting on the back porch and all of a sudden Anthony got down on one knee and proposed to me. I was so happy and super surprised, I said yes! I just kept staring at the beautiful ring that he placed on my finger. Anthony had asked my father for my hand in marriage before then and was given the blessing. My dad joked, "Why not? You already got her pregnant!" Even though my relationship with Anthony wasn't the greatest, we loved each other the best we knew how.

I gave birth to a healthy baby girl in March of 2006. When my father visited our house after we went home from the hospital, he said that there was so much pink that it looked like someone threw up Pepto Bismol everywhere. He made sure that he arrived the day she was born to be one of the first people to meet her. It meant a lot to me that he continued to want to have a place in my life and in the lives of my children. He had been a wonderful grandfather to our oldest son, so I knew he would also be one for our daughter. It felt so good to have him around and active. It also brought us closer together.

Anthony and I lived together in low-income housing. The stress of two kids and bills weighed heavily on us. We argued a lot about everything; I was miserable and I knew he was too, even though he would always try to convince me that he was happy. The only way I can explain it is that we were so comfortable with each other and never truly evolved into an adult relationship. We fought like cats and dogs. It was an emotional roller coaster, and as a result, I would soon find myself vulnerable in some situations.

In June of 2006 a few months after our daughter was born, Anthony started a new job at the automobile factory that his father worked at. It was a great job making really good money. We actually both applied and submitted our applications on the same day but I wouldn't start until a couple of months later in mid-August. I really liked my new job, and I loved the money. The only problem was that I had enrolled in college for fall classes and because of my work schedule and being on a probation period for 90 days, I had to drop all of my upcoming classes for the semester. I never did go back, money was more important than school at that point.

Working with the same people all day, every day for 10 hours straight, you get to know them and hear their life stories and gossip about their families both good and bad. That's kind of how it started when I met a certain guy that happened to be 14 years older than me. I was 21 and, even though I had been through a lot, you could stay I was still pretty sheltered when it came to being street smart. I was also very gullible, partly because my mother controlled my life for the most part because I allowed her to. I didn't know any different. It wouldn't be long before he would be sitting with me at lunch and we would talk about our relationships. I considered him a friend; he obviously had been in the game 14 years longer than me, so he knew exactly how to reel me in and was really good at it, unfortunately for me. I began to let my guard down because I was unhappy and had someone that was really interested in me. I felt wanted and not rejected like so many times before in my life. Unfortunately, I didn't know what I was opening myself up to.

I started working out trying to get all of the left over baby weight off of me, so I was losing some weight. He noticed and would compliment me and compliments go a long way for someone who is craving love and attention – both of which I was not receiving from my fiancé. It stemmed back to even further than that to me not having my father around when I was growing up, and a direct result of not feeling unconditionally loved by my father. Knowing what I know now, Anthony or my new friend couldn't fill that void for me, nobody could but God.

This other guy was married with three kids. He had been with his wife since they were 17 and he wasn't happy and looking to get a divorce. He let me know that he slept on the couch every night and it was just a matter of time. He was such a great guy and the stories he would tell me about what he was going through with his (then) wife were pretty crazy and I sympathized with him. By this time, I had opened the door to having an emotional relationship with him, so I was already at the point of no return. It wouldn't be long before the relationship progressed to more than just being emotional, and I found myself in a place where I had no clue how I got there. I watched my mother go through this with her cheating husband being with another married woman, and I said I would never do anything like that, but here I was becoming my own worst nightmare.

It was December 2006, right before Anthony's birthday, and I told him that I no longer loved him, didn't want to be with him anymore, and that I wanted him to leave MY townhouse. In my mind I felt like I was doing the right thing before it went any further with this other relationship that I had begun. I was somehow, in my twisted way of thinking, helping Anthony by being morally correct. Well, as much as I could, considering the situation. I remember him sitting on the bathroom floor with the engagement ring I had given back to him in his hands just crying and pleading with me to change my mind and to make it work. I was so cold and had a mental folder of all the reasons why I not only would not, but could not, continue to be with him. I made up my mind that I was done, and that he could no longer make me happy. I watched him gather some things and he left back home to his parent's. It was hard for me to do, but I knew that I didn't want to live like this anymore and that I had greener pastures coming my way, so I thought.

Bella was 9 months old and a complete daddy's girl from the moment we brought her home from the hospital. Matteo was four and had only known his mother and father together. I tore our little family apart. I heard stories of how Anthony had lost 20 pounds in the matter of a few weeks, and how depression had kicked in. I didn't let that stop me; my heart was so hardened to him because of the constant bickering. I was also very selfish even after everything we had been through, I didn't want to look back. The "greener" lawn I had decided to play on was not what it was made out to be, but I would be blind to it for a while. The other guy still lived at home with his wife but would soon file for divorce and move out on his own. It's sick how happy I was to see someone else's marriage fall apart so that I could be happy. You will never be happy under those circumstances and the foundation that our relationship was built on would eventually crumble as a result. Our coming together would also tear his family apart.

When my mother found out about what was going on, and that I was seeing a married man, she came to my house after finding a picture of us together at a bar and the visit ended in a physical fight. I called the police on her. My mom had a lot of practice with these situations from her own cheating husband and her sister's. My mom decided to take it upon herself and go over to his wife's house and tell her everything. She told her how he was having an affair with her 21 year old daughter. His wife wasn't surprised though, this had not been his first rodeo! After I found out about the visit, I told my mother to stay out of my life and that I was never talking to her again. After the police were called and came to my house to take pictures because of the assault, I agreed to drop charges so that she wouldn't lose her state licensed daycare, but reminded her that I didn't want anything to do with her. More than six months would go by before my mother and I would even say a word to each other. During this time, Anthony was still around my family because they all loved him, even my extended family. I still allowed my mother to take care of my kids while I worked, but we didn't speak to each other except through my little brother and sister. It was awful.

My life was a complete mess, but with this new adventure I was on, I was completely oblivious to it. The whole time I was with this other guy, which was about two and a half years, Anthony wouldn't give up on trying to get me back. He would even try to bear hug me so I couldn't get out of it. I wanted nothing to do with the past chapter and relationship in my life. This other guy was really good to me, but I always sensed he played games and there were many empty words said. I chose to ignore the red flags because I thought he really loved me and he showed it the way I thought love was supposed to be shown, but it was tainted. The foundation of our relationship was built upon lies, adultery and lust. Talk about a rocky foundation!

We had been through a lot together; his ex-wife, needless to say, was not a fan of mine and had plenty of bad things to say to their children anytime she saw me. His teenage daughter would have two children and make him a grandfather twice during our time together. My kids really liked him and he liked them, too. We would go places and do a lot of family things. I was content and very "happy." Anthony seemed to be moving on with his life, also. After having some fun when he was done drowning in his sorrows, he ended up in a relationship with a girl who also had two children. They moved in together, broke up, and got back together again. She had her own issues, was very jealous and insecure, and had Anthony in bondage to her own oppression and depression. Things were going really well with my boyfriend until I found out I was pregnant. This wasn't the same as when I found out I was pregnant the other three times; I was happy but the feeling was overshadowed by being afraid of what people would say. At this point, my mother and I had been in the process of mending our relationship. She let bygones be bygones and sacrificed her own opinion for a relationship with me. I was a little nervous about what my boyfriend would say; after all, he was already a grandfather and was about 37 years old and I was only

23. During the week after I broke the news to him, he was shocked, and then he embraced it. We even had a girl's name picked out and everything, then the next thing I knew, I was sitting in an abortion clinic frozen in time. I couldn't believe this was me doing something that I've always been completely against. It was his idea and I did it because I felt like if I didn't he would leave me and I didn't want to be left alone with another child and have two different baby daddies. It was selfish, I know, but I couldn't see past my current feelings and situation.

That experience was a blur, but not quite the blur I had hoped for. I was sitting in the waiting room with other girls at 7:00 a.m. I looked at their faces and wondered what they were in for. I was looking for the stories written on their faces (as if I didn't have a story of my own) or better yet, maybe we are all there for the same reason. They called me back, it was my turn. I was sitting on a table and a nurse came in and did an ultrasound. I was eight weeks, I could see the tiny speck on the screen. I can't believe I was able to follow through with it even after seeing my baby. Looking back, my boyfriend was my stand-in father figure and all I wanted to do was please him, even if it meant losing me in the process.

After that, the doctor came in. He explained what would be happening and turned on a machine that sounded like a vacuum. It was loud, and as I laid there, tears were streaming down my face like a river. I was damaged goods. When the procedure was done, and the life was sucked out of me I went to a nice little room with cookies and juice because somehow that would make things better; what a lie! I sat there crying and crying. The nurses were trying to comfort me, handing me tissues and offering pats on the back after I had just killed my baby. The life that was growing inside of me was precious. I went home, walked past my mother who I was currently living with and went back to bed. I would wake up different on the inside, but to the naked eye, I appeared the same - or maybe I didn't.

It was May, the Saturday before Cinco de Mayo, a huge Mexican celebration with a parade. I was so hurt on the inside but I disassociated myself with what happened earlier that morning and wouldn't come to terms with it for quite a while. I took my kids and sister to the parade. We had fun and took lots of pictures. I've looked back at them once and when I look at myself I see emptiness, but it's amazing what you can portray to everyone else who has no idea where you were earlier that day. I hadn't heard from my amazing boyfriend all day since he dropped me off after our little visit to the clinic. I called him and there was nothing, he didn't ask how I was doing...nothing. One thing I knew is that nothing would ever be the same. That day, I lost yet another piece of myself.

Chapter

6

The Chains are Broken

Psalm 30:2-3

Lord my God, I called to you for help, and you healed me. You, Lord, brought me up from the realm of the dead; you spared me from going down to the pit.

Much like a slowly deflating balloon that was my relationship with Anthony, the same thing was now beginning to creep into every area of my life. I was hurting inside and having fun with all the wrong people and doing things I just didn't quite feel right doing. One thing is that my boyfriend was not controlling, which most people expected with the age difference. It was actually the exact opposite. Most people would think that being younger myself would cause him to keep me at arm's length, but he actually had no problem with me hanging out with my girls and going to bars and clubs and occasionally he would join us. Coincidentally, I would hang out with girls from Anthony's high school that he grew up at. I can clearly remember one night going out with a couple of girls to a biker after hour's club on the wrong side of town. It was a whole different world from what I was accustomed to when going out. For starters, it was basically a small building (probably an old house) filled with men and half-dressed girls looking for the wrong attention. There were cars lined up and parked in the middle of the one way street right in front of the club. We had to park three or four blocks down from the club. That was scary in itself because of what side of town we were on. I was just waiting for a guy to jump out of the bushes and snatch us. Although I was curious, I had no good feelings inside of me about where we were headed but, I was with my girls so I followed. Once we actually got in, it was pure evil, the way the men were looking at not just me but all of the girls there. They were sizing us up almost looking for their prey. I watched this one group of guys talking about this girl that looked promiscuous and completely intoxicated as she was grinding with one of their friends. They made sexual motions of positions he could put her in. I almost puked and was even more scared. Although I was in this ever dangerous situation, I wasn't a dummy. My mom always talked to me about being aware of my surroundings and never drinking anything someone brought to me, or if I did put my drink down, never pick it back up. She watched plenty of shows about how guys would spike girl's drinks with date rape drugs and she didn't want me to fall into that trap. I always tried to be aware of my surroundings and no matter how much I tried to fit in, there was just something that would always pull me back and sober me up. Even with all of that training, somehow I was in this very dangerous position. I really had to go to the bathroom and my friends were dancing with guys, so I went alone. I had to wait in a long line, while being gawked at by the women that were giving me looks as though they were asking, "Why are you here?" The men were also looking at me like, "Can I take you home?" NO absolutely NOT! Finally I got in the bathroom, and even though I was behind the door, I was afraid because the door lock was crappy and I was afraid that taking down my skirt to use the bathroom would make me way more vulnerable to rape but I really had to pee. Again, even though I wasn't in church, I still remembered how to pray and I did, I prayed that God would protect me. It was probably one of those, "God please get me out of this situation unharmed and I'll do anything" type of prayers. I made it out of there without anything horrible happening after I convinced my friends I was ready to go. That was the last time I went out like that ever again. I know that God protected me from my bad choices because anything could have happened. That's the thing about God's love and grace is that even though we get ourselves into bad situations, when we call out to God and surrender, he will help us get out. He's a good father.

Back on the home front, I was not who or where I wanted to be. My life had spun out of control whether I was the only one who could tell or not. The way I lived my life at this point in time was completely out of my character. No, I was never perfect, but even in high school my friends would be experimenting with different things that I could never do. I'll be honest, it's not that I didn't want to do it too, something would just stop me. I began having nightmares and feelings of evil all around me, I was being demonically attacked. I was scared, couldn't sleep and was constantly praying the best way I knew how. My grandma used to pray with me every night whenever I would sleep with her and those prayers were still there when I needed them. It was like learning to ride a bike, it's something you never forget. I prayed, but after a few restless nights, I couldn't take it anymore. The best way to describe it would be when you're watching a cartoon and the character has an angel on one shoulder and a devil on the other. That's what was happening to me. I had crazy thoughts and tried to think different things and nothing worked, I was being tormented in my mind and I would soon find out the mysterious ways in which God works.

My boyfriend transferred to a different plant in the beginning of our relationship. However, I still remained. Working at the automotive plant, I met all kinds of people from different walks of life, ages, and backgrounds. You have no choice but to talk to them or your shift will pass very slowly. I swore like a sailor and one day while working next to the plant chaplain, I was told, "You're such a beautiful girl to have such bad words come out of your mouth!" That really pierced me and planted a seed that would later be watered. Another person that I talked to quite often was a Christian man. He always invited me to church, but was never pushy. He always read his Bible at lunch and on breaks. I would later realize that the seeds that he would plant in my life he would also help water. One day, I was put in his zone outside of my ordinary job. Everything weighed so heavily on me and I couldn't take it anymore, I just broke down and started crying. I looked up and I saw him, he was like a beacon of hope and light that God would use to bring me to Him. I was led over to him crying and pouring my heart out like he had asked me to tell him my life story. He surprisingly knew exactly how I felt and began to give me his testimony of how God brought him through his circumstances and saved him. I so desperately wanted that too, I wanted to be saved! He told me everything he could in that little bit of time and gave me a plan of action. He told me I needed to go to church and invited me to his. He assured me that God loved me and wasn't mad at me and that He would meet me right where I was in life. I had to ask him, though, if his Pastor could tell if there were evil spirits possessing me because of the constant darkness I felt around me. He said yes, and that he would pray with me. That all sounded so great and gave me hope.

This all happened the week leading up to Labor Day weekend in 2008. My boyfriend and I went on a trip to the West side of the state to visit his brother's family. It was really nice where they lived, but I was so uncomfortable. All I could think about was getting back home in time to go to church on Sunday. My boyfriend didn't think we'd make it back and if we did, he wasn't planning on going with me, but that was not going to stop me. On the way home, I called the guy from work to let him know I would be there. He actually wasn't planning on going to service that night. I was bummed. Then he called me right back and said he would be there because that was like inviting someone to your home and then not being there when they arrived. I was excited inside, and I was in great expectation of what would transpire going through the doors of the church that evening. I had no idea what to expect, but I was ready.

We got back into town, and I went home and put on my nicest club clothes and headed to church. As soon as I walked in, I was greeted by a really nice lady with a huge smile. She was very welcoming and it was like I was in the twilight zone because I had an overwhelming sense of complete peace. I don't think that I have ever felt so peaceful. That woman ended up being my coworker's wife. He then greeted me and sat me where his wife was going to sit once the service started. I sat there with their children, listening to the instruments in complete excitement at everything that was going on around me. It was like my senses were magnified; sensory overload at its finest. Then the woman on stage began to lead worship, and as soon as the music started playing, I stood up and began to weep. I could feel the love of God saturating my very being; it was moving through me inside and out and all around. I knew He was there, God was there. I had an appointment that I just found out about just a couple of days earlier but God had it on the books even before I knew my own name. At the end of the service there was what I now know as an altar call. If you wanted to be saved then that was the time to go up and declare Jesus as your Lord and Savior. I went up without hesitation. As I stood there in God's glorious presence, I cried.

The Pastor began to speak over my life as though he knew me and my thoughts. The Holy Spirit used him that night to truly show me the power of God. After I received Christ, I headed back to a room where I had to wait for someone to come in and talk to me about how to get started in my faith and walk with Christ. Minutes felt like hours, and I began to get a little squirmy and heard things in my head like, *okay it's time to go you can fill out this paperwork another time and it's time to leave.* I was thinking of excuses to get out of there and quick. Just as I was getting up to tell them, "Thanks I'll be back to do this another time," someone came in and I knew it was too late. You see, the most wonderful thing just happened to me but the enemy knew that if he could get me out of there without solidifying and being accountable to my next steps as a believer, I may have brushed off my experience. Instead, I stayed and learned about all of the ways I could grow, and as a result, God began a healing in me that evening, not because He couldn't do it before, but because I was now ready to receive it. I was on fire for the Lord and this was the perfect church because they were open just about every day of the week. Whenever they were open, my children and I were there. I attended the beginner's Christian class on Monday, Bible study on Tuesday, then worked in the nursery for Bible study on Wednesday, choir practice on Saturday and Sunday school along with three services on Sundays. People would tell me it didn't take all of that, but it did for me - every last bit, they had no clue what I had been through.

About a month after I had been going to church, my boyfriend began to show interest and eventually he would bring his children. He was right there with me at every service and Bible study. It was great because we were doing it together. I had my eye on the prize. I surrendered myself to the Lord from day one, all I wanted was to know my purpose and do God's will for my life. I was growing quickly and things were beginning to fall off of me. I was so hungry for God's word and power in my life. They are not kidding when they say knowledge is power. The more I read my Bible, attended church and sought God's face and will, the more understanding I received. Things were being uprooted out of my life and I was happy to let them go because I wanted everything that God had for me. There were evident changes, even in the things that seemed small. After coming home for weeks, excited about what I learned in church and re-preaching the word to my mom, she finally visited the church. The first time she came, she wasn't fully prepared to receive. She came back though, and eventually joined the church. Things were finally starting to come together. My prayers were being answered in ways I wasn't expecting.

My boyfriend and I would hand off the kids every other weekend to our exes. The weekends happened to fall on the same weekends for both of us so when we didn't have the kids, we would spend the whole time together. On those weekends I would stay after work Friday through Sunday at his apartment. During the week, I would usually stay one night with him. That slowly began to change though, it didn't feel right anymore. I knew better, so I wanted to do better. I started the process of obedience in all things. I soon stopped the mid-week slumber parties. Before I knew it, I would stay only one night during our weekends together and pretty soon I stopped staying overnight all together. After the abortion, I was on a five-year birth control because I didn't want to get pregnant by him again. I would finally make up in my mind that I was done with sex outside of marriage and went and had my IUD removed. My doctor asked me why I wanted to do that and I told her it was because of my beliefs. I know that sounds crazy but it's not as spiritual as you think. It was simply because I was no longer going to have intercourse because I wasn't married. Up until that point, my boyfriend was handling the changes well, but he would also try to tempt me and a couple of times he succeeded. Overall, I was doing better than I was a month earlier. After those couple of slip-ups I made the decision to not spend as much time there, period.

At the end of January 2009, my pastor led a church-wide fast for 14 days. I felt led to cut out all distractions and journal. I told my boyfriend that I was going to take that time to really seek God for His direction and my purpose. I wanted to be in His presence and I wanted everything He desired for me. During that time, I would write in my journal every day recording the beauty that The Lord spoke to me. I would only see my boyfriend at church during this period and I was fine with it, but he had a rough time. Fasting is powerful and God really broke some things off of my life and brought clarity in the midst of me seeking Him. The fast truly served its purpose. God began to speak clearly about some decisions I needed to make.

From the time the kids and I started going to church until that point, there were a lot of things happening in the spirit that were beginning to shift into the natural. God was working behind the scenes! I had a few discussions with Anthony about how radical I was and how he thought I was taking my walk with Christ a little too far. Anthony thought I was a little out there in left field because all of a sudden I was "sold out" for God, going to church five days a week. It did open the opportunity up for me to be able to give him my testimony and to plant seeds about God. One night, I read him a few chapters in a book called Divine Revelation of Hell and explained that so many people are deceived and there really was a hell. He actually received what I was saying to him over the phone, but I don't think he was completely convinced. One night while praying with my kids, they asked "Mommy is daddy going to go to hell because he doesn't go to church like we do?" It was so sweet and innocent and the looks on their faces were of sincere concern. I didn't know quite what to say but immediately I told them that we were going to pray for their daddy's salvation so that he will give his life to Jesus and go to church. So every night from that point on at the end of our prayers, we would pray for their father's salvation. They would squeeze their eyes so tightly when we got to that part and Jesus would soon answer their prayer, but in a way none of us imagined…

The kids and I invited him to church one Sunday because they were singing in the children's choir. He came, surprisingly, and sat in the same row - right next to my mother. I was honestly happy he was there, it meant a lot to the kids, but more importantly it allowed God to soften his heart. My boyfriend wasn't very happy, but that's not what was important. I remember having to hold his hand during service just to feed into his man hood and take away some of his insecurity. Anthony didn't stay for the whole service but at least he was open to come and see his kids. I would later find out that after Anthony visited our church, he talked to his girlfriend and asked her if she would go to church with him. Once she confirmed that she would never be caught in a church, he said that he knew he wasn't going to be with her for good. God was already beginning to move but I was not yet aware of it.

Almost immediately after the fast ended, I heard the Lord loud and clear in my heart say that my boyfriend was not "The One" (my husband). Before this point, I truly thought he was. I thought we were going to get married and live in a house with all of our children and just be the Brady Bunch. As hard as you would think it was to be obedient and walk away from my relationship, I did not hesitate. I knew that I had heard God correctly. I was willing to surrender everything to the Lord including my relationships. I called my boyfriend almost immediately and told him that I needed to talk to him and that I was on my way over. When I got to his apartment he looked sad like he already knew what I was going to say. We went to his room, shut the door and sat on his bed. I told him that I couldn't be with him anymore and that God was leading me in a different direction and I wanted His will for my life. I let him know exactly what The Lord revealed to me and that I had to be obedient. Surprisingly he took it very well and didn't have much to say besides he felt like God was also speaking to him at that moment telling him to leave the church we went to together. I figured that he felt like that's what he needed to do and I wasn't going to argue. I told him thank you for everything and said goodbye. I left his apartment feeling amazingly free, and when I got in my truck, the song "I Am Free" by The Newsboys greeted me. At that point, I knew that God really did have a great sense of humor.

I don't think it hit him right away because it wasn't long before he texted me and he even called once before I changed my number and I answered. He told me he loved me, and that he planned on proposing to me the following week on my birthday and he had already told his family. I told him I was sorry, but it was over. I had to follow God and He was taking me in a different direction. With not many tricks left up his sleeve, he said I've been thinking about how I want to have a baby with you. I was screaming inside because of what he had talked me into previously that ended with me killing our baby. Instead of getting upset, I read him a piece of a book about a lady that visited Heaven and saw the babies that were aborted and miscarried. She saw their spirits leaving hospital rooms and being put in beautiful baskets by angels and the angels taking the basket to the throne of God and placing it on the altar. She then saw God stick His hand in the basket and make them whole. In her book she wrote that God said if their parents will turn from their ways and follow me, they will one day be reunited with their children. I thought that was beautiful and I cried as I told him. That was the last thing I ever told him as he tried to comfort me, but I no longer needed his comfort because I realized that my Father in Heaven sent the Comforter.

Chapter

7

Restoration

Matthew 18:21-22

Then Peter came to Jesus and asked, "Lord, how many times shall
I forgive my brother or sister who sins against me? Up to seven
times? Jesus answered, "I tell you, not seven times,
but seventy-seven times."

For the next couple of months, I felt like I was in seclusion. I was reading many different books and studying God's word continuously, spending precious quiet time in His presence. I loved every minute. I had already been redeemed and made righteous through the blood of Jesus Christ when I invited Him to be the Lord of my life, but there are many different layers of healing and God wanted to fully restore me. He wanted to restore my whole being from the inside out. Anthony knew from the kids that my boyfriend and I had broken up, but he never tried to use that as a way back into my life. I appreciated that. All he did was remind me he had said it would only last two years, and he was right. From the point that he found out about our relationship to then it was exactly two years. There were a lot of other things that he would blurt out in the short period of time I would drop the kids off or pick them up while I was still with my boyfriend. I never confirmed them for him at the time, but he was usually spot on and I never understood how he knew. Everything would soon start to make sense.

My mother also was on fire for the Lord teaching children at our church, singing in the choir and little by little being healed and restored. God began to make the ashes of her life beautiful. We served together in this ministry and it was wonderful. God restored our relationship, it took time, and wasn't always an easy process. We are still strengthening it to this day, but when I look at my mother, I don't see the person she once was, she has been made new through Christ. I have forgiven her just like Christ has forgiven me. She is a pillar in my life and she constantly lifts me up in prayer because she is a warrior and God uses her to stir up my gifts. Besides my husband, she is my biggest supporter and I love her for that!

My relationship with my father was going well for a long time. I believe that it was able to stay afloat for so long because it was very surface. We tip-toed around the elephant in the room, and never talked about past hurts and disappointments. We avoided them actually, it was safer that way - or so we thought. You can only do that for so long before the past comes rearing its ugly head. In order for healing to come, you have to deal with issues of the past, there really is no way to get around it. Suppressing your feelings will only work for so long and will cause chaos and turmoil within.

The issues came to a boiling point some years later and would cause such a great rift in our relationship, and all of the progress that had been made would disappear in an instant. This blow-up incident involved truth to be spoken along with words that would cut deep and would be hard to recover from, but not impossible with God. The truth is that we both have to want a relationship enough to move past what happened. It recently hit me that in order for this restoration to happen, it needed to be me that reached out. This was somewhat difficult because in my mind I felt like we had to lay this out on the table before moving forward but I also realized that was "my idea" of the way our restoration should occur.

God commands us to honor our parents and I knew that if I am to truly serve the Lord with all of my heart, mind and soul, then I needed to humble myself and honor my father. No matter what, I love my dad and realize more than ever that in place of hate or anger, compassion fills my heart for him. Knowing bits and pieces of his story, I get it, but it doesn't take away the pain or rejection I faced growing up. I do thank him for doing the best he knew how to. I don't blame him completely, and I realize that God's grace is also sufficient for him. I believe that when you are a certain way for so long unless you begin to admit where you are and what you do you cannot begin the healing process within yourself - let alone with others. I pray that he too will truly receive the love of Christ, which is the only true unconditional love. Without that love, you cannot know what it means to truly love others.

I pray that he also receives complete healing from the inside out. I pray that he be released from any generational curses or words spoken over him that are not of Christ. I pray that he be released from any guilt of past mistakes in marriages, relationships, and fatherhood. I forgive him and I love him and I know one day that our relationship will be fully restored and I will continue to stand on that promise. I know that in God's timing, and not my own, restoration will happen.

I have also forgiven my stepfather, and I am no longer angry at him. I can do the simplest things that were previously a chore like being able to say his name. The feeling of disgust and puking doesn't cross my mind when I see his face. God even encouraged me to go even a step further in my healing and his. God had been healing me from the inside pertaining to the abuse I suffered from my stepdad. He had been preparing my heart for not only complete forgiveness, but compassion toward my abuser. I also knew that in order for my step dad to move forward in his life, I had to let him know that I forgave him. This did not happen overnight by any means, but was definitely a process. Leading up to the time that this meeting of forgiveness would happen, God put him in my path. I saw him two times within a couple of weeks' time. The initial time was at lunch when I was with my two youngest children, my sister (his daughter) and my mom. He came up to the table and gave my children money. The next encounter was at a fish fry that Anthony and I went to. We were in line getting ready to pay and my stepdad got in line right behind us. When it was our turn to pay, we realized that they did not take debit cards but only cash. We told the cashier that we would go to an ATM and return afterward. My stepdad interjected and handed the cashier enough money to pay for our lunches. Anthony and I said thank you; we were very grateful. I realized that the time was drawing nearer to the point where I knew God was calling me to share my forgiveness.

About a week after he paid for our lunch, my step dad had been in the hospital with some health issues. I didn't think much of it until one early morning I couldn't sleep. I woke up around 5:00 a.m. and then woke Anthony up. I let him know that I felt like the Lord wanted me to go to the hospital to release my stepdad from the guilt and shame and let him know that he was forgiven. Anthony simply said, "You have to do what you have to do." That's all I needed to hear. I began to pray and ask God for the words to speak. I asked Him to lead me and that His will be done in my life and the life of my stepdad, and in turn, God would be glorified through this encounter. I worshipped and prayed all the way to the hospital. As I sat in the parking lot, I felt an overwhelming feeling of joy. I knew that I was going to be used as an instrument to set my stepdad free. Free indeed. I walked into the hospital which happened to be a Christian facility, and as I got to the floor where his room was located, I got nervous and headed into the bathroom. I prayed for the strength to do what God was calling me to do. Then, almost immediately, someone came on the intercom announcing that it was Morning Prayer time. I bowed my head over the sink and prayed. When it was finished, I walked down the hallway. I could see the parallel from when I did my walk of shame years earlier to let him know I hated him for what he did to me the previous night. This time, I was doing a walk of freedom and letting him know how much God loves him. Wow!

Outside of the room, there were two nurses doing their morning rounds. I asked them if my stepdad was alone in the room and they said he was. I thanked them, and walked right passed the room to the window at the end of the hallway. I gazed out to see the beauty of God, and worked up my nerve to go in the room. It was time; I walked up to the door and knocked. I heard him tell me to come in. As I opened the door and gazed into the room, the look on his face was not surprised. Had God been preparing him too? I walked in and sat down as though I had an appointment. I guess you could say I did: a divine appointment to be exact.

One thing you have to realize is that before this moment, we had not been in that close of proximity for more than a few minutes for more than 10 years, and here I was sitting at his bedside like an old friend. I asked how he was doing, and we talked about how great of kids my little brother and sister were (his children), and other small talk. That was all great, but I was on a mission from God and it was time to complete what God sent me to do. I began to tell him about how God had changed my life. I began to share some of my testimony and how in spite of my imperfections, God still loved me, forgave me and called me to Him. I spoke to him about the cross and how Jesus died for our sins before we even came to know Him. I began to tell him how what he did to me affected me. But I also let him know that nothing but the love and grace of God could have brought me there that day to let him know that not only was he forgiven by me, but God can and will forgive him too.

He listened intently as I spoke about God and gave my testimony until the moment when he said he was sorry. I told him that if he wanted to do anything for me, it would not be to give my kids money or to buy my lunch, but it would be for him to forgive himself. I asked him if he had a relationship with Christ and he let me know that he did and had been going to church. I asked him if I could pray with him, and he said yes. I grabbed the same hands that had once hurt me and began to pray over his life.

Among many things, I prayed that guilt and condemnation would be cast out. I prayed that he would use his influence as a business owner to lead people toward Christ and that God would be glorified through his life. I prayed that from that moment on he would never be the same. It was amazing. When I was done, I gave him the biggest hug and whispered, "God Bless you" and "I love you." I left the hospital overflowing with love and joy in my heart knowing that I answered the call.

As far as my teenage babysitter that first abused me and was used by the enemy to try and break my spirit at such a young age, I have no idea where she is in the world. I believe that she too may have fallen victim to sexual abuse. This situation has been a little different in the healing process because it was hidden for so long underneath the memory of a three-year-old who didn't realize what was happening at the time. I do forgive her, and pray that God heal her from the inside out and that the sins of her past are not lingering and consuming her.

I saved the best part for last. A few months went by after my ex and I broke up. I would see Anthony for our trade-off with the kids and that was about it, until one day he came to drop them off and when I looked at him, my heart began to race. I felt something overwhelming that I couldn't quite put my finger on at the time, but it was nice. The next thing I knew, Anthony and I were playing one-on-one basketball in my mother's drive way like the good old days. I know that my family and our kids must have been a little shocked and confused about what they were witnessing but not as much as I was! He left shortly after our little game of one-on-one, and we said goodbye. That was the most interaction we had experienced in two years and that was completely my choice. I wanted to talk to him when he left, I wanted to hear his voice, and more importantly, I wanted to know what the heck this feeling was, so I called him. The first and only thing I could think of as a way to call him and spark up conversation was to ask him when he was taking the kids for his summer visitation, how awkward was that?

"Why did you do that?" Anthony asked.

"Do what?" I replied.

"Let me be around you?"

I didn't have an answer, but God did. He would later tell me that He allowed me to see Anthony through His eyes and not my own, so that's why I felt the love for him that I was feeling. Before this point when I saw Anthony, I wanted to run. All that was engrained in my head when I thought about him were our past experiences and they were not always pretty. I wanted nothing to do with that, there was no way I was ever going back. As a matter of fact, I even told him that before when he let me know that my boyfriend and I were only going to be together for a couple of years. I said, "Well even if that's true, I will still never be with you!" I was confident that we were finished for good. There was no love there as far as I was concerned. God on the other hand, had completely different plans.

The day that Anthony and I played basketball together was also the day that him and his girlfriend decided to put a down payment on a house that they were going to rent together. By the next day after our experience he had already let her know that he couldn't be with her and that she could keep the deposit money and ended their relationship. At that point, there was no rekindling being talked about, he just felt like he knew it was already over and must have realized that. He came to church soon after, and gave his life to Christ, and then prayed to God to have his family back. It was amazing, and God spoke very clearly, assuring me that Anthony was my husband. We were leaving JC Penny's one day and as we put our stuff in the car a voice out of nowhere said "You two are a match made from Heaven." A man began to speak over our lives and let us know that God had ordained us to be together and prayed that what God put together no man could tear apart. It was so awesome because he was a complete stranger. I had never seen him before that, and haven't seen him since.

Within a month or two of Anthony coming to Christ, we were engaged to be married! He proposed to me right after church and it was perfect. We got married seven months later on February 12, 2010 in a beautiful, intimate ceremony. I married my best friend and the love of my life. Although I have the security of knowing that Anthony is who God ordained for me to spend my life with, it has by no means been easy. There are many things that we have had to overcome; big and small. We will always have interferences that will keep us pressing in and seeking God for strength and wisdom in our marriage. One thing that is for sure is that there is a difference now than when we tried it the first time around not connected to Christ. God is the center and He's leading the way. We had two more beautiful children to complete our little family. There is a nine year age gap between our oldest and youngest and we wouldn't have it any other way. I thank God for his healing and restoration power, and most of all, for second chances. I thank Him for His unmerited and undeserved favor-grace! I didn't deserve a second chance. I didn't deserve to be forgiven, but my Father says otherwise because of who He is and not what I've done. I have the greatest team in the world with my Creator by my side and my best friend. God is a God of restoration!

Chapter

8

Unashamed

Isaiah 50:7
Because the Sovereign LORD helps me, I will not be disgraced.
Therefore, I have set my face like a stone, determined to do his will.
And I know that I will not be put to shame.

This part of my story ends here, but the start of a new set of chapters in my life has begun. Throughout all of the uncertainty and chaos, one thing was for sure: I could only go up from there. Healing is a layer-by-layer process. The key to this process is forgiveness. I had to not only forgive others, but forgive myself. Without forgiveness, it's like you're secretly being poisoned, little by little, and dying a slow death, most times not even realizing it. The ironic part is that you're doing it to yourself. Forgiveness is not only to release the other person, but to release the burden of carrying the pain yourself. You should never give anyone that much control in your life besides Christ. In the midst of forgiveness, you also need to understand that God is not the culprit of any of your pain. In Psalm 145:9, it says "The Lord is good to everyone. He showers compassion on all of His creation." This scripture doesn't say God is good to some and sprinkles compassion on a few. He's good to EVERYONE and showers compassion on ALL of His creation! He is a good God, so only good can come from Him. I could have easily tried to blame God for the unfair things that happened in my life. I realize that in the same way, God patiently waited at the doors of my heart knocking like a gentleman calling me to Himself. He never barged in because I had my own free will. This is the same way He waits at the door to everyone's heart until they make a decision to let Him in. Some open that door, some will open it in the future, and some choose to always leave it closed. Despite our decision, we are all given this opportunity for Salvation. It's called The Good News of Amazing Grace!

No matter what we have done, are doing, or will do, He still loves, wants, and calls us, waiting with arms opened wide. This is important because when you understand this, you will understand that when Christ is not invited to live inside of you, the enemy of your soul (who, by the way, isn't a gentleman) will barge right into your life and set up camp, and unfortunately has legal right to operate in your life. If The Holy Spirit is not leading and guiding you, then your flesh is ruling you. In John 10:10, the Bible says,

"The thief comes only to steal, kill and destroy; I have come that they may have life and have it to the full." You are the "they" He is talking about in this scripture. You can find many examples of Satan at work in my life, and just like God uses people, he can use them as well. He used people to steal my innocence, hope and relationships. Even greater than that is you can also see God's redeeming power at work when I decided to receive Him into my life and fully surrender. It all boils down to choices, so don't blame God for things that have happened in your life that resulted in rotten fruit, because God can only create things that bare good fruit. God can turn anything around, all of your hurt and pain and make a beautiful masterpiece out of it. He will allow you to use your story as a testimony that will end up helping many others. My testimony will never be in vain: if it saves one life or brings healing to five, it was worth reliving all of it because it brought me healing also.

When you have God by your side, what the enemy means for harm will be turned around and used for God's glory. Once you are at that place where forgiveness spiritually and naturally collide, the healing process will begin. The ball and chain that you realize you no longer have to carry can't hold you down from moving forward anymore because in Matthew 11:30, it says, "For my yoke is easy and my burden is light." You are freed from all of the toxins and poisons that tried to pollute your mind and cloud up your vision. You will come to a place where you are unashamed. Your testimony becomes a treasure and treasures come in all shapes and sizes but are all equally important to The Father. Our God cares about details such as how many hairs are on each of our heads. When you have a treasure, you don't keep it to yourself, because you know that it's better to give than to receive. You and your treasures alike are God's precious gifts to the world not meant to be kept for ourselves. You can then move past the perceptions of others, and be courageous like the Bible says in Deuteronomy 31:6, "Be strong and courageous. Do not be afraid or terrified because of them, for the Lord your God goes with you; He will never leave nor forsake you."

It takes courage to be unashamed before God but once you receive His Grace and unconditional love, being unashamed before man is a piece of cake. When you are unashamed, you can be a voice for God to help those who are and have gone through what you and God together have already conquered. Today is a new day - this moment is a fresh start. I pray that you take this opportunity to take a risk! Ask The Lord to search your heart and reveal to you places, people, incidents and things you need to forgive. Remember, if you are a child of God you are courageous so you can do it with the help of His spirit inside of you. It's time to let go of the past hurts and pains whether they are self-inflicted or not eagerly received. What do you have to lose? If you are thinking to yourself that you can't seem to move forward in life, or feel like something is holding you back, cry out to God. The Bible says in Mark 2:22, "And no one pours new wine into old wineskins. Otherwise, the wine will burst the skins, and both the wine and the wineskins will be ruined. No, they pour new wine into new wineskins."

Therefore your past may be holding you back from receiving the newness that Christ has for you. You can't move forward if you're looking in the rear view mirror. You can do it, I believe in you, but more importantly so does God. He says in John 16:33, "I have told you these things, so that in me you may have peace. In this world you will have trouble. But take heart! I have overcome the world." If you don't have a relationship with Christ now, or you have never completely surrendered and everything in between, you're up! All of this is for you, but first you need to take a step in the right direction, and it begins with having faith smaller than a carrot seed. The Bible says in Matthew 17:20,"Because you have so little faith. Truly I tell you, if you have faith as small as a mustard seed, you can say to this mountain, 'Move from here to there,' and it will move. Nothing will be impossible for you."

A mustard seed is one of the tiniest seeds there are - even smaller than a carrot seed. At one point I hadn't seen one, but I had seen a carrot seed. They are also pretty tiny. Mustard seeds are even smaller than them. The point is that in order for nothing to be impossible for you, you only need a small amount of Faith. With that faith, you can accept The Lord Jesus Christ as your Savior, believing that he died on the cross for payment of your sins and rose from the dead three days later.

If you're ready to accept Jesus Christ, here is a simple prayer that you can pray right this moment: Lord Jesus, I ask you to forgive my sins and save me from eternal separation from God. By faith, I accept your work and death on the cross as sufficient payment for my sins. Thank You for providing the way for me to know you, and to have a relationship with my heavenly Father. Through faith in You, I have eternal life. Thank You also for hearing my prayers and loving me unconditionally. Please give me the strength, wisdom, and determination to walk in the center of your will. In Jesus' name, Amen.

My prayer for you as you have shared in my personal testimony is that you took the opportunity to allow God to be the Lord of your life. You will experience love and peace like never before. If you are unsure or even just a little curious, then ask God to reveal Himself to you. If you took the leap of faith then congratulations, you did it!! You took the first step and God will honor you for that. Welcome to the family! All of the angels in Heaven are rejoicing! God Bless You on this new journey that you will embark on whether you have decided to let go of past heartaches and pains, renew your relationship with Christ or just begin your relationship with Christ through faith. The key to who you are and what you're entitled to can be found in the Bible. I pray that God will send divine connections and relationships that will help grow your knowledge in Christ. You have been redeemed!

Through the redemption I have received through Christ, I have received my new Blueprint:

You reached your hands out of the sky so that I wouldn't die

Die without a purpose and live a life feeling worthless

Your love has covered me

It has healed me emotionally

To you I appreciate the love you use to saturate

Only you can deliver from the unthinkable

Before I knew you some memories were awful

I was abused and terrified of the things I saw when I closed my eyes

Only you can come down and begin to release

Your love that will surround

Covering me with your Grace as if I could see you face-to-face

My heart was broken but you took those ashes and made them a token

Your Holy Spirit guides me even when others around despise me

I know that what I stand for isn't always popular

I'm not concerned about that because you're the one who builds my rapport

For you I will stand

Following the guidance of your hand

For you I will stretch

Even under any pressure that may erect

I'm like Abraham, that couldn't stay in his comfortable land

He had instructions to follow to the place that held his overflow

Obedience is Key and Faith unlocks

The things you have in store will knock off socks

You're loyal and constant and I will always be grateful

For the day you pulled me out because you knew I was able

Able to be trusted with the lost here on earth

You set me apart because you knew I would take back turf

My heart, my spirit and my body are yours, so begin to use me as if you were using yours

I'm able, I'm ready

It's time to be steady

We have so many things to do for your Kingdom

I wanna be so close to you that I can hear you breathin'

You are my Savior, my God, and Creator

I stand up now to fulfill every endeavor

Given to me by you

Through your word that breaks through

Every bondage and every curse

The weapons you give me will immerse

Let's do it now, continue to show me how

I'm locked and I'm loaded and ready to wow!

Chapter

9

Experiencing Freedom

Psalm 118:5
Out of my distress I called on the Lord; the Lord answered me
and set me free.

You may have heard the statement that freedom isn't free. In order to be free from something, you had to have gone through a process to gain your freedom. The definition of freedom is the state of being free, or at liberty, rather than in confinement or under physical restraint. When you are not free, you are restrained and in bondage to whatever burdens are holding you down, and back, from being all that God has created you to be. God says in His word that you are more than a conqueror, you are strong and courageous, you are the head and not the tail, you are above and not beneath, and you are created in the image of our heavenly Father!

Once you receive Christ as your Lord and Savior, and have begun your road to healing and forgiveness, it's time to walk in the freedom and purpose that has been designed for you. The enemy of your soul would like nothing more than for you to carry around anger, resentment and unforgiveness, If he can get you to continue your pity party by magnifying the wrongs that have been done against you, then you will be way too consumed with that to focus on the one who can heal you from the pain of your past or present situation. Trust me, I know. Remaining defeated can be a full-time job in itself, not bringing you any closer to the victory that awaits you.

When you give your life to Christ, and invite Him in to cleanse you, there is something supernatural that happens. Your sins are washed away, and you are reborn and welcomed into the family of Jesus Christ. Although this wonderful thing happens initially on the inside, all of your cares and concerns do not disappear immediately. You still have your flesh that is similar to memory foam and does not quickly forget what it has been accustomed to. You will still have to walk out life's obstacles. If your marriage was on the rocks before you received Christ, your marriage will be on the rocks directly after, but it's not over! You will have the power that will keep you fighting. You will have wisdom available to you to help you turn things around if you depend on Christ and not on your own understanding. Best of all, you will have the Holy Spirit that is like your own personal GPS to help you stand on the hope and promises of God.

In John 14:26, it says, "But the helper, the Holy Spirit, whom the Father will send in my name, he will teach you all things and bring to your remembrance all that I have said to you." It is your job to feed your spirit with the word of God, and it's the Holy Spirit's job to bring it back to your remembrance when you need it. God gives you a spiritual heart transplant when you surrender to Him. Your heart is no longer hardened, but softened like a heart of flesh. In Ezekiel 36:26, it says, "I will give you a new heart, and I will put a new spirit in you. I will take out your stony, stubborn heart and give you a tender, responsive heart."

Your heart will become more like Christ which is a heart of love and compassion for all of His creation. The key to growing more like Christ is by spending time in his presence and reading His word. Have you ever hung around someone, whether it be a spouse, coworker, or even a friend, and you begin to pick up their verbiage or quirky habits? I have, and it's because you spend a lot of time in their presence. It's the same thing with God; the more time you spend with Him, the more your heart and ways become like the Father's. This process is called sanctification, which means becoming more like Christ. This process will not end until we are in eternal glory with the Father. Along the way, we will make mistakes and fall short, but we can get back up and keep pressing forward. The purpose of having the Father's heart and love is evidenced through 1 Peter 4:8, which says, "Most important of all, continue to show deep love for each other, for love covers a multitude of sins." When Jesus walked the earth and performed miracles of healing and deliverance, He was always moved first by compassion like in Matthew 14:14, where it says, "Jesus saw the huge crowd as he stepped from the boat and he had compassion on them and healed their sick."

As believers in Christ and heirs to the throne, we too have the same power to heal and deliver. The same power that spoke this world into existence lives within you and I. In Romans 8:11, the

Bible says, "The Spirit of God, who raised Jesus from the dead, lives in you. Just as God raised Christ Jesus from the dead, he will give life to your mortal bodies by this same spirit living within you."

That is powerful news! You have the power by the testimony of your mouth to raise people's dead situations and spirits back to life. This is an amazing opportunity to be an ambassador for Christ. I once heard this statement and it will always remain in my life's mission: Rescued people rescue people. Think about that, if you have been rescued out of spiritual, physical, or emotional slavery and are experiencing freedom from those giants in your life, then compassion should move on the inside of you to be used by God to help rescue others so they can experience freedom.

In 1 Corinthians 10:31, it says, "So whether you eat or drink, or whatever you do, do it all for the glory of God." The whole point of everything we do in life is to glorify our Heavenly Father. That's what we were created to do. We can give Him Glory by being Christ-like, by giving Him honor and praise. One of my favorite call-to-actions in the Bible is the Great Commission. In Matthew 28:16-20, the Bible says, "Then the eleven disciples went to Galilee, to the mountain where Jesus had told them to go. When they saw him, they worshiped him; but some doubted. Then Jesus came to them and said, 'All authority in heaven and on earth has been given to me. Therefore, go and make disciples of all nations, baptizing them in the name of the Father, and of the Son, and of the Holy Spirit, and teaching them to obey everything I have commanded you. And surely I am with you always, to the very end of the age.'"

God has not asked us to go out and make disciples – followers of Christ – He has commanded us to. Ever since the fall in the Garden of Eden when sin entered the world, the enemy has worked hard to take as many souls to hell with him as he can.

In 1 Peter 5:8, it says, "Be alert and of sober mind. Your enemy the devil prowls around like a roaring lion, looking for someone to devour." He understands that because of the victory on Calvary when Jesus was crucified on the cross for you and I, bearing all of our sins as a perfect and spotless sacrifice, and was raised from the dead, the enemy's clock began ticking.

In Colossians 2:13-15, the Amplified version of the Bible says, "When you were dead in your sins and in the uncircumcision of your flesh (worldliness, manner of life), God made you alive together with Christ, having freely forgiven us all our sins, having canceled out the certificate of debt consisting of legal demands against us and which were hostile to us. And this certificate He has set aside and completely removed by nailing it to the cross. When He had disarmed the rulers and authorities (those supernatural forces of evil operating against us), He made a public example of them (exhibiting them as captives in His triumphal procession) having triumphed over them through the cross."

The enemy knows that his time will soon be up. When Jesus said on the cross, "It is finished," He meant it. In Revelation 20:10, it says, "Then the devil, who had deceived them, was thrown into the fiery lake of burning sulfur, joining the beast and the false prophet. There they will be tormented day and night forever and ever."

A price has been paid in full for you, me and every single person in the entire world. Salvation is a free, but not always easy, gift. That is why we, as the Body of Christ, need to function. Each of us represents a part of the body. So, it's up to us to be in line and functioning properly (not perfectly because there was only one who walked this earth who was perfect), so we can help weaker members of the body begin to function. Open your mouth and be a mouthpiece for Christ, open your home and be a safe place for people to be able to grow in the things of God, build a home for a family in need to show the love of Christ with no strings attached, or do something as simple as giving a stranger a warm smile. Even the little things go a long way.

I pray that you will allow God to use you each and every day, and shine through you. I pray for divine appointments when you can be an encouragement and a beacon of light and hope to someone who so desperately needs to know they are seen. I pray that God blesses you to be a blessing to others. You have a purpose, you have a destiny, and you will, through Christ, complete all that God has planned for you before you were knitted in your mother's womb.

In Psalm 139:13-16, it says:
For you formed my inward parts;
You knitted me together in my mother's womb.
I praise you, for I am fearfully and wonderfully made.
Wonderful are your works, my soul knows it very well.
My frame was not hidden from you, when I was being made in secret,
Intricately woven in the depths of the earth.
Your eyes saw my unformed substance; in your book were written, every one of them,
The days that were formed for me,
When as yet there was none of them.
In Jesus mighty name, Amen!

I charge you, fellow brother and sister in Christ, to be a trailblazer and to go into your circles of influence to be the representative for Christ you were called to be. It is an honor to serve together with you as we serve our Father in Heaven. There is no end to this story, just a continuation of my story for His glory!

2 Corinthians 1:3-4
Praise be to the God and Father of our Lord
Jesus Christ, the Father of compassion and
the God of all comfort, who comforts us in
all our troubles, so that we can comfort those
in any trouble with the comfort we ourselves
receive from God.